2020
G/A 5494216

2020
G/A 5494216

SONY

digital
editable
recordable MiniDisc

**The In-Car MiniDisc. It only
skips when you want it to.**
The Sony MiniDisc in-car system
with ^Digital Sound Quality, Instant
access to your favourite tracks,
Shock Resistant Memory to
avoid skipping, flip-out panel for
security, Joystick Commander,
which enables you to keep your
eye on the road and a Rotary
Encoder that replaces the buttons
for volume, bass, treble and fader.
We haven't skipped anything
you wanted to hear, have we?

http://www.sony-europe.com

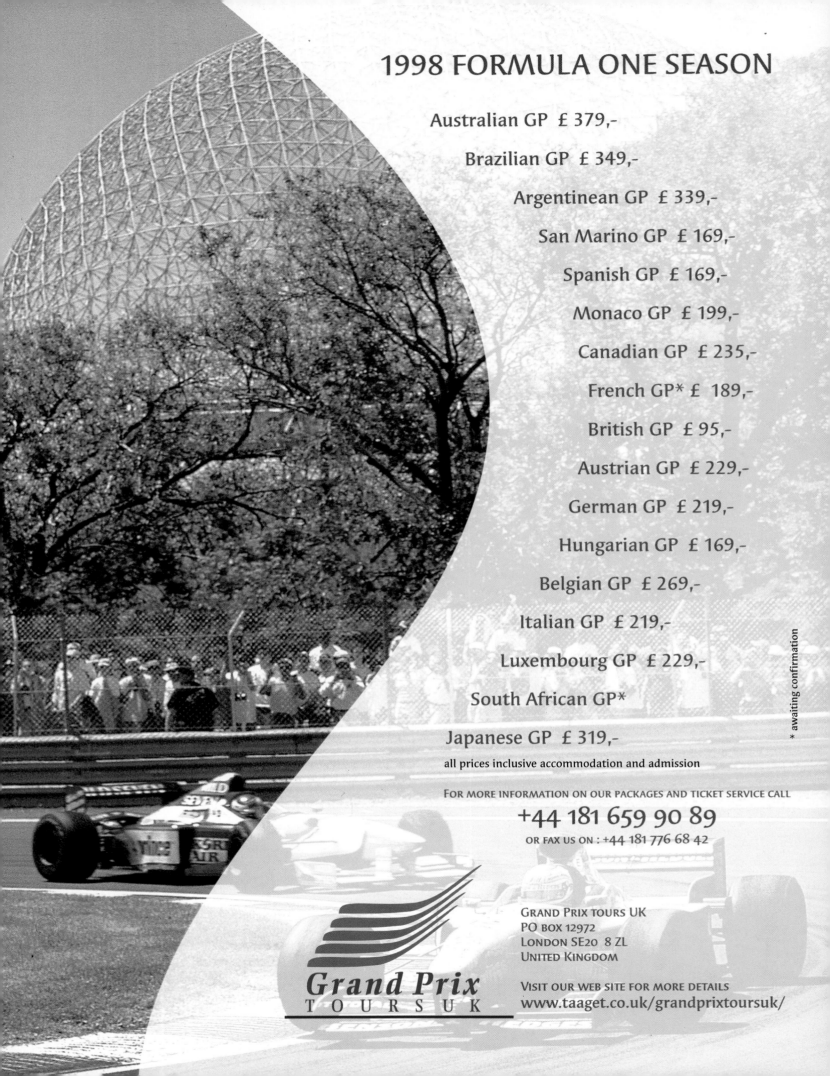

F1-50
5, Ella Mews
Cressy Road
London, NW3 2NH
UK

Tel : + 44 (0) 171 428 7010
Fax : + 44 (0) 171 284 2118

http://www.F150.com

F1-50 Council Members
John Cooper
Patrick Head
Stirling Moss OBE
Alain Prost
Jackie Stewart OBE
Professor Sid Watkins
Frank Williams

Publishers
Peter Antell
Jonathan Feld
The Apex Group, London

Project Director
David Woods

Editor
David Tremayne

Contributing Writers
Gerald Donaldson
Tony Dodgins
Mike Doodson
Mark Hughes
Joe Saward
Helmut Zwickl

Marketing
Billy Brown
Andy Hanson
Anthony Stone

Production
Colin Davidson

Administration
Sabine Schmitz

Art Direction
Siren Design, London, SW1

Design & Production
The Conservatory, London, NW3

Translation
Context, London, SW14

Photography
Phipps Photographic, Diss, Norfolk

Public Relations
Judith Hunt, JHC, London

Distribution
Comag

Printed in Italy

Contents

Introduction 5
The Official World Championship is born - Silverstone 1950 8

Overview : Reign of the maestro **10**
The Top 10 drivers 14
M is for Mercedes and Marketing 15
Personalities : - Enzo Ferrari, Tony Vandervell, Alfred Neubauer, Raymond Mays .. 17
Five Great Races 20
V is for Vanwall and Victory 21
A legacy of common sense - John Cooper's rear-engine revolution ... **24**

Overview : Technologically fertile **26**
The Top 10 drivers 30
The Cosworth DFV 31
Personalities: - Colin Chapman, Rob Walker, Louis Stanley 33
The case of the sailor's head 34
Five Great Races 36
Wings and things – aerodynamics hit F1 37
The milk and water man - Jackie Stewart's crusade for safety **40**
Driving all four wheels 43

Overview : The Multi Coloured Circus **44**
The Top 10 drivers 48
The birth of ground effect 49
Personalities : Mauro Forghieri, Keith Duckworth, Luca di Montezemolo, Gordon Murray .. 51
Five Great Races 54
Turning up the boost – the dawn of the turbo era 55
Niki Lauda - phantom pragmatist **58**
Radical radials – beating the prejudice 59
Lording it up – Hesketh Racing 61

Overview : A decade of growth **62**
The carbon cocoon – carbon fibre technology 65
Immovable object , irresistible force - Alain Prost & Ayrton Senna .. **66**
The Top 10 drivers 70
The return of pit stops 71
Five Great Races 72
Turning the key – the dramatic success of Williams 75
Personalities: - Frank Williams, Bernie Ecclestone, John Barnard, Jean-Marie Balestre, Ron Dennis .. 77
Changing circuits 78
The red & white steamroller 79

Overview : A theatre of controversy **80**
Overtaking, what overtaking? 83
The Top 10 drivers 84
Personalities: - Max Mosley, Patrick Head, Flavio Briatore, Prof Sid Watkins, Tom Walkinshaw .. 87
The fastest athletes 89
Five Great Races 90
Refuelling : playing with fire? 91
Red revival 93
F1 : non-contact sport or boxing match ? **94**
The rise & rise of Williams 95

Statistics 98
World Champions and World Champion Constructors, Greatest number of wins - teams & drivers
Wins per season - teams & drivers, World Champion engines
Greatest number of pole positions - teams & drivers, Greatest number of fastest laps - teams & drivers
Greatest number of Grand Prix participations - teams & drivers

Team profiles 102
Arrows, Benetton, Ferrari, Jordan, McLaren, Minardi
Prost, Sauber, Stewart, Tyrrell, Williams

Into the future - Catia's F1 design revolution 116

At 9:32 am on 12 November 1991, after a four year labour, the Honda NSX entered the world.

Weighing a healthy 3014 lb 6 oz, it was the child of Formula 1, conceived in the pits, with Senna, Mansell, Piquet and Prost for godparents.

It was not a difficult birth, as it came during a decade in Formula 1's 50 year history almost entirely dominated by Honda.

Between 1986 and 1991, Honda won all six F1 Constructor's Championships and five consecutive Driver's Championships.

Working with both the Williams and McLaren teams, Honda engineers kept setting the standard for speed and reliability. Not bad for a car manufacturer largely known for producing cars more like the Civic and Accord.

Throughout their involvement in Formula 1, however, Honda's racing and production engineers were planning a supercar, the New Sports Experimental, or NSX.

Honda wanted to harness their Formula 1 knowledge to offer the public a vehicle with the raw power of a racer refined for the street.

It would be as close to driving a racing car as you could get without needing ten years of training to actually handle it.

At the heart of the first NSX was a 270 bhp 3 litre V6 VTEC engine that came directly from Honda's racing experience.

As did almost every aspect of the car.

How else could Honda have developed a street car capable of 0-60 mph in as little as 5.7 seconds and a top speed of 167mph?

Also developed in Formula 1 were its lightweight titanium connecting rods, race car suspension, computerised traction control and F-matic transmission, controlled from a finger-tip stalk on the steering wheel.

And, like F1 cars, it had a remarkably lightweight yet incredibly strong body. In fact, it was the first all-aluminium production car in the world; a feat that would have been impossible without our F1 involvement.

Perhaps, next Mother's Day, a certain Formula 1 racing car will be getting a big bunch of flowers from a grateful NSX.

If you would like any further information, call 0345 159 159.

Technology you can enjoy, from Honda.

Mother!

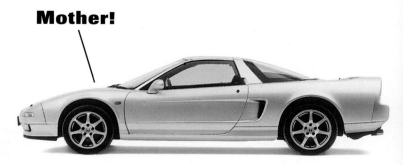

Introduction

The FIA Formula One World Championship is the greatest form of motorsport, the pinnacle of technological perfection and endeavour, the aspiration of every race driver worth the name. F1.50 is a celebratory look at half a century of this great series, as we have sought to place the disparate eras into perspective.

Grand Prix racing resumed almost immediately after the war when on September 9 1945, on a circuit in the Bois de Boulogne near Paris, the French staged the Robert Benoist Trophy race for cars under one and a half litres, which was won by Amedee Gordini. The Liberation Trophy for two litre cars was won by Henri Louveau, while Jean-Pierre Wimille, then the greatest driver in the world, won the Coupe des Prisonniers in a four point seven litre Bugatti. Of necessity, the cars were all leftovers from another era.

In February 1946 the Paris-based Association Internationale des Automobile Clubs Reconnus (AIACR), the governing body of motor racing, changed its name to the Federation Internationale de l'Automobile (FIA), and delegated the government of the sport to its offshoot, the Commission Sportive Internationale (CSI). Its most urgent task was to establish a new formula, bearing in mind the exigencies of wartime shortages and the need for industry to rebuild. Normally aspirated four and a half litre cars had not been able to get anywhere near the supercharged three litre cars in 1938 and '39, so now the ratio between supercharged and unsupercharged engines was changed from 1:1.5 to 1:3, and the new formula would cater for cars with one and a half litre supercharged engines, or four and a half litre normally aspirated power units. Essentially, it was what would have been introduced in 1940 had the war not intervened.

It proved a success, and in 1947 F1 started to get back on its feet with Alfa Romeo, Maserati and Talbot contesting the races and the Alfettas in particular threatening to match the speeds of the mighty pre-war Mercedes. 1949 was less promising, with Alfa Romeo taking a sabbatical, Ferrari's promised supercharged V12 engine failing to materialise until the end of the season and the much-vaunted BRM V16 continually being delayed, but 1950 was a landmark.

In 1949 the Federation Internationale Motorcycliste (FIM) had staged the first motorcycle World Championship, and for 1950 the FIA followed suit, reviving a concept last used in the Twenties. Seven races - Grands Prix in Britain, Monaco, Switzerland, Belgium, France and Italy, plus the Indianapolis 500 in America, would form the World Championship. Drivers could count four out of seven scores, and points were awarded on the basis of eight for first, six for second, four for third, three for fourth and two for fifth. Whoever set fastest lap got an extra point.

The series kicked off at Silverstone on May 13 1950, with the British GP. Giuseppe Farina, who rather fittingly would go on to win that inaugural World Championship, triumphed for Alfa Romeo from team-mates Luigi Fagioli and Reg Parnell, the other points going to Yves Giraud-Cabantous and Louis Rosier in their Talbots. Farina also took the point for fastest lap.

When the FIA conceived the new Formula One back in 1946, and the World Championship four years later, it can never have envisaged just what a global impact it would have, but it was the start of something big.

Here then are the stories of the greatest marques and the greatest races. But while the technology rightfully has its place, this is essentially an intensely human story, one of competition, success, weakness, strength - and tragedy. The span of years marking the 50th anniversary of F1's birth has created a chance not just to remember those who won, but to salute those who fell yet, in doing so, wove something indelible into the fabric of a fabulous sport.

Our celebration of five decades of motor racing unequalled in any other category, is told by top Formula One writers. It is our sincere hope that you enjoy reading it as much as we have enjoyed researching, reporting and writing it.

David Tremayne

Harrow 1998

PUMA
A DRIVER'S DREAM

■ 1.7 litre Zetec SE variable cam timed 16v engine ■ 125 bhp ■ 0-60 in 8.8 seconds ■ Just a few

British GrandPrix
1950

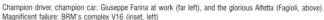

Champion driver, champion car: Giuseppe Farina at work (far left), and the glorious Alfetta (Fagioli, above).
Magnificent failure: BRM's complex V16 (inset, left)

Following the lead of the governing body of motorcycle racing, which had introduced a world title in 1949, the FIA deemed 1950 to be the inaugural world motor racing championship year. In reality the contest comprised just six European Grands Prix and the only loose way in which it could be considered a 'world' title was the inclusion of the results of America's premier race, the Indianapolis 500, an event contested by totally different drivers, teams and types of cars.

Nonetheless, it was a beginning, the watershed where motor racing properly emerged from the shadows of the war. In recognition of this significance, Alfa-Romeo re-entered the sport it had withdrawn from the previous year. Its car was a pre-war design, but that was hardly important at the time for its participation brought much-needed prestige to the series. At that time, few outside of racing knew much of Ferrari, then in its infancy as a Grand Prix constructor and of the big pre-war hitters, the German Mercedes and Auto-Union teams were not yet in a position to consider participation.

The very first event of the new series was the British Grand Prix, held at Silverstone on May 13th, a Saturday so as not to impinge on Silverstone village's Sunday service. This was a tradition of the Northamptonshire track which was to last into the late Seventies. In honour of it being the inaugural event, the race also carried the title of 'European Grand Prix'. It was a sunny spring day and the chance to see the giants of the sport in action brought out a huge crowd, estimated at around 100,000, to the converted wartime airfield, bringing the surrounding roads to a complete gridlock. The venue itself could

barely cope either; gate personnel were overwhelmed and many were able to get in free of charge.

Also spectating for free were the Royal Family, with King George VI present and introduced to the drivers before the event by Britain's top representative Reg Parnell, having a one-off outing for the Alfa team in support of regular drivers Fangio, Farina and Fagioli. The King was accompanied by then-Queen Elizabeth, now Queen Mother.

Twenty one cars lined up for this historic race, though it was hardly a closely competitive grid, 18 seconds separating poleman Giuseppe Farina's practice time from that of the slowest competitor, Belgian band leader Johnny Claes in his Lago-Talbot. Ferrari had not readied its cars in time for the event and so behind the dominant Alfettas on the grid were an assortment of pre-war ERA 'voiturette' racers and converted sports cars such as the Talbots. Many of the star names on the grid were familiar to pre-war racing enthusiasts; as well as Thirties Alfa driver Farina, there were Luigi Fagioli, Louis Chiron and Philippe Etancelin, all major players in the decade before the war.

The circuit used Hangar Straight for the pits area, the cars then turning sharp right and up the runway before rejoining the more familiar part of the circuit. As the flag was dropped it was Juan Fangio's Alfa which made the running but eight laps from the end he retired with engine failure, thus handing the race to Farina who led his other team-mates Fagioli and Parnell to an Alfa 1-2-3. The result was the cornerstone of what was to be Farina's world title.

It hadn't been a great, closely-contested race - the Alfas circulated in team order and were two laps ahead of their nearest rival at the end - but it was the beginning.

Mark Hughes

Reign of the Maestro

Grand Prix racing had existed for 44 years before the World Championship was officially instigated in 1950 and in many key areas it had changed little during that time. It was still largely the preserve of 'factory' teams - manufacturers whose business of producing road cars funded their race programmes -it was still dominated by continental Europe, and the cars still carried their engines at the front.

Yet just a decade later, the structure was fundamentally different in all of these areas. The might of the factories had been overthrown by tiny specialist companies, 'garagistes' as the traditionalists sniffily referred to them. Britain had become the motor racing capital of the world. The winning cars were mid-engined. All the pieces were in place, in other words, for the F1 of today; all bar the commercialism at any rate. It was a decade of astonishing change; change which arrived from a surprising direction, one borne of thrift.

And it was the teetering economic health of post-war Europe which led indirectly to the FIA's inauguration of the first Drivers' World Championship. It was a move designed to help firm up the faltering steps the sport was taking after the devastation of war.

Six years after Farina's Silverstone triumph for Alfa Romeo (pictured above with Fagioli) the changing face of the F1 car is reflected as Fangio's Lancia-Ferrari takes the flag there in 1956 (left).

'It was a decade of astonishing change, which arrived from a surprising direction, one borne of thrift.'

It gave Grand Prix racing a public coherence, rather than the appearance of a random series of stand-alone events. It gave a nod to popularism by acknowledging that drivers were more likely to capture the imagination than machines, particularly the tired assortment of pre-war clunkers that comprised the early post-war grids. And in prefixing the title with World, the governing body was displaying the international - rather than European - aspirations it had for the sport.

Regardless of its hopes for the future, however, the field which took the flag on May 10th 1950 at Silverstone was nowhere near as impressive as those which routinely gathered in major Grands Prix immediately before the war. Indeed, it was roughly similar to a pre-war, sub-GP, voiturette field. Which was not so surprising, given that the Grand Prix formula (Formula One)

in place since 1946 was loosely based on that of the old voiturettes. It allowed for supercharged engines of up to 1.5 litres or - in order that the post-war grids could be bolstered by adaptations of existing sports car engines - normally aspirated 4.5 litre units. It was not the most glorious or technically exciting of Grand Prix formulae but it was practical, tailored to the straitened circumstances of the time and, with the help of the new World Championship campaign, it worked... for a while.

Alfa-Romeo's exhumed voiturette Alfettas dominated the first two years of the championship. When the points were totted up (8, 6, 4, 3 and 2 points for the first five places plus one for fastest lap), pre-war ace Giuseppe Farina was the inaugural World Champion. Pre-war driver, pre-war cars, but the future could not be denied indefinitely. Not only was post-war discovery Fangio Alfa's World Champion in 1951, but the supercharged Alfettas had met their match in the new normally aspirated 4.5 Ferrari.

Realising that it had squeezed its last drop of success from a 15 year-old design and without the resources to replace it, Alfa withdrew from the series. Unfortunately F1 was not yet strong enough to survive such a loss. It left Ferrari with a strong, post-war design way faster than the assortment of old voiturettes and converted sports cars which comprised the competition.

The answer - to make the World Championships of 1952 and '53 comprise races for F2 cars (2 litre normally aspirated) - may not have been a spectacular success in that Ferrari (with Alberto Ascari) dominated regardless. But it was an answer that to the perceptive hinted at the future. The pattern was unmistakable: pre-war Grand Prix cars had been replaced by smaller voiturettes which in turn had given way to yet smaller F2s. Perhaps the sub-F2 cars pointed the way ahead?

Those wishing for a glimpse of that needed to look to the recently introduced low-cost F3 which was proving a wow in a Britain now spoiled for choice of race

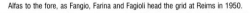

Alfas to the fore, as Fangio, Farina and Fagioli head the grid at Reims in 1950.

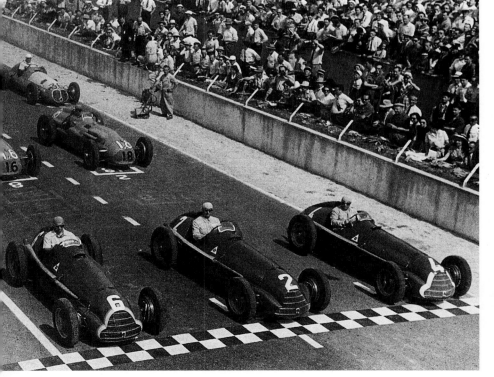

Moss heads his Mercedes for victory at home, Aintree 1955.

Jack Brabham's end-of-decade Cooper (bottom) provides a dramatic index of F1 progress when compared with the prewar ERA and postwar Maserati above.

circuits cheaply converted from wartime airforce bases. Of course the World Championship could never be for weedy 500cc motorcycle-engined cars like these, but the design concept - mid-engined out of convenience for the chain drives - and the growth of UK race car expertise that this junior formula had initiated, would ultimately exercise a profound effect on the big picture.

It was a movement whose time had not come quite yet, but it wouldn't be long. While the new wave of British design and driving talent sharpened its teeth on such nursery slopes, the big-time players on the continent, not seeing what was coming, had become complacent.

For the FIA's new-for-'54 2.5 litre Formula One, Ferrari and Maserati produced classic designs which were effectively little more than bigger-engined updates of their F2 cars, while Mercedes-Benz re-entered the sport with a crushingly thorough but essentially classical car. Such support made for a healthy championship from a sporting perspective - heightened by some nationalistic fervour as Mercedes added another nation's colour to the racing red of Italy, the blue of France and the green of the occasional British underachiever - but technically it was a period of excruciatingly slow development.

Fangio took a couple more titles as the best driver in the best-engineered car (Mercedes) and thereafter, following the three-pointed star's withdrawal in light of the 1955 Le Mans tragedy, a couple more as the best driver in cars no worse than anyone else's (Ferrari and Maserati). The period even saw a new British challenge - Vanwall - but this was not part of the grass roots movement that was bubbling under. Rather it was a one-off from a rich industrialist, joining at the top, intent on beating the continentals at their own game, but playing it in the same vein.

The big factory teams, fat on success, had become vulnerable without their even suspecting as much. Some of their representatives were probably even unaware quite what the funny, tiny, apparently crudely constructed car with its proprietary engine at the wrong end was when they saw Stirling Moss practice it at Argentina 1958. They surely would have known after the race, because it won.

The underclass had arrived, courtesy of Cooper and the 500cc F3 movement. The proud reputations, the in-house engineering of every major component, the previously puny record of British cars in Grand Prix racing, all counted for nothing. Within 12 months little mid-engined Coopers, using off-the-shelf engines and gearboxes, but designed and constructed with the shrewdness borne of a decade in the burgeoning British racing scene, would be dominating Grand Prix racing more surely than even Alfa-Romeo or Mercedes ever had.

And Cooper was just the start. There were others - ultimately more permanent - in the same vein on the way. But that is jumping ahead a little. Because, although the movement had arrived, it had not yet taken over. In hindsight the 1958 season was the passing of the baton from old to

Hawthorn, Britain's first champion, heads for second at Spa in 1958.

new, from red to green. Fittingly, Fangio chose to retire early in the season, feeling he had no part to play in the coming age of the 'green cars'. No Fangio and funny little kit-cars winning Grands Prix? The sport would never be the same again.

But tradition would have its last stand nonetheless. Ferrari was strong and despite Cooper's stunning start the little cars still needed further development before they were capable of sustaining such form - as they were to do in 1959 and '60. No, the sustained challenge to Ferrari in 1958 would come instead from Vanwall, a sort of half-way house between old and new; British and with lots of the very latest aeronautically-inspired technical detail on the one hand, but still front-engined, built in-house and well-funded on the other. There was none of the financially imposed make-do ingenuity of Cooper about Vanwall.

It was fitting that the retirement of Fangio coincided with a separate World Championship for constructors for the first time. Fitting, because it had previously seemed that whichever team the maestro drove for would win. Now, with the playing field levelled, the idea of a champion constructor suddenly had more meaning. But regardless of whether Ferrari

or Vanwall would take this inaugural honour, it was a safe bet that the champion driver would be British. Ferrari's weapon against the Vanwall line-up of Moss (who was only in the Cooper in Argentina because Vanwall had given the race a miss) and Tony Brooks was the pairing of racing mates Mike Hawthorn and Peter Collins.

The British driving talent borne of the new wave had attained Grand Prix success much earlier than the machinery. Moss was an instant thorn in Mercedes' side in his first full season in 1954 with a privately-entered Maserati. Hawthorn had by this time already been a Ferrari driver for a year - and taken his first Grand Prix win in sensational fashion at Reims as far back as 1953, when he beat Fangio in a wheel-to-wheel battle. Furthermore, any discussion of the world's top six drivers in the wake of Fangio's retirement and Ascari's death would also include Brooks and Collins. So it was that towards the end of the Fifties Britain was supplying the leading drivers and cars after half a century of contributing neither. Until Brooks triumphed at Syracuse in 1955, the nation's leading proponents in Grand Prix events had been de Hane Segrave and Kenelm Lee Guiness in the Twenties and Dick Seaman, briefly, in the late Thirties.

The history books record that it was Vanwall which took that first constructors' title in 1958, Hawthorn the drivers'. Honours even between red and green. But it was the last season in which there would be this focus on national colours. The pragmatism of Cooper's age transcended patriotism - it gained its success largely with Antipodeans Jack Brabham and Bruce McLaren and even Moss' Coopers were finished in the dark blue of private entrant Rob Walker. There was less a feeling of racing for Queen and Country than racing as a commercially viable wheeze, and rather enjoying upsetting the Establishment in the process. It was, unwittingly, the change in emphasis which would later allow the sport so seamlessly to embrace commercial sponsorship.

It was also, perhaps, the beginning of an era which would never again see the level of sportsmanship evident in 1958. Consider that Hawthorn was initially disqualified from the Portuguese Grand Prix for an alleged push-start and that he had to rely on the eye-witness account of a fellow driver in his appeal against this decision. Then consider that this other driver was his title rival, Moss. Had Moss kept quiet, Hawthorn would have been deprived of the points that would later prove so crucial as he beat Stirling to the title. Mention it to Moss today and his view remains precisely the same: 'It would have been utterly unthinkable to have done anything else. Mike had not done anything wrong and didn't deserve to be penalised.' The sporting act of a king who did not need to wear a crown.

Then think forward to Senna vs Prost at Suzuka in 1990 or Schumacher vs Villeneuve at Jerez in 1997. F1 had indeed become a very different world.

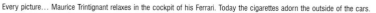

Every picture... Maurice Trintignant relaxes in the cockpit of his Ferrari. Today the cigarettes adorn the outside of the cars.

The Top 10 Drivers

Mark Hughes

1. Juan Manuel Fangio

You simply cannot argue with five World Championships and 24 Grand Prix wins in just seven complete seasons. And all this from a man who was already 39 when he began his F1 career…

Fangio's all-round talent seemed almost mystical. His knack of keeping out of trouble, of never looking anything but unflustered, and the reserves of blinding speed that could be called on when necessary- such as at the Nurburgring in 1957 - suggest an ability that was often barely being tested.

He was certainly the greatest of his generation and in an era when the driver could make so much more of a difference than today, the team that succeeded in signing him would be virtually assured of the crown. This is attested by the fact that his five titles were taken with four different teams - Alfa-Romeo, Mercedes-Benz, Ferrari and Maserati. Yet none of this seemed to detract from the man's supreme grace and humility. 'You must always aim to be the best,' he said, 'but you must never believe that you are.'

He retired, aged 47, mid-way through 1958, as reigning World Champion.

2. Stirling Moss

That a driver this great never won the title simply undermines the stature of the World Championship. For from the time Fangio retired in July 1958 up until the accident at Goodwood in April 1962 which brought Moss' career to an end,this man stood head and shoulders above his contemporaries. Speed, adaptability - he won in Maseratis, Mercedes, Vanwalls, Coopers and Lotuses - cunning, he had it all.

A loyalty to British teams undoubtedly compromised his final tally of achievement, but that matters hardly at all when one considers how routinely he could transcend the limitations of his machinery.

Rising from the ranks of 500cc F3 in the early Fifties to instant F1 competitiveness in a privately-entered Maserati in '54, he spearheaded a new wave of British drivers – one which, for the first time in the history of the sport,

had a central role to play in Grands Prix. Patriotism saw him combine forces with Vanwall, where only his sportsmanship lost him the 1958 world title, and for the next three years he gave displays of genius virtually every time he climbed aboard the cars of the private entrant Rob Walker.

3. Alberto Ascari

The first successful second-generation Grand Prix driver, Alberto was six years old when his father Antonio was killed racing for Alfa Romeo in the 1925 French Grand Prix at Montlhery. In the early Fifties he was the only man consistently on the same planet as Fangio, and took consecutive world titles for Ferrari in 1952 and '53.

Sheer speed was the strongest colour in his paintbox - Hawthorn reckoned him to be 'even faster than Fangio,' though Moss disagrees with this - and when he got out in front, his was a sublime skill via which his absolute dominance simply seemed to break the opposition. He was less impressive in adversity, however, when he had a tendency to desperation, and then it was usually the machinery that he broke.

A man obsessed by coincidence and his father's fate, he was killed in a testing accident at Monza in 1955. He was the same age to the month that Antonio had been in his final race.

4. Jose Frolian Gonzales

This huge bull of a man gave Ferrari its first championship Grand Prix win when he defeated Fangio's Alfa Romeo at Silverstone in 1951. He took a further win there in 1954, the year in which he was runner-up to Fangio in the championship. But after a relatively short career he returned to his homeland of Argentina, where he remains today.

He could physically dominate a car to

great effect and on an 'on' day he was electrifying. That day at Silverstone, for instance, he completely overshadowed his team-mate Ascari. He was as strong as an ox and had stamina to spare – significant in an age where Grands Prix lasted considerably longer than they do today.

But Gonzales's was not a cultured technical skill in the way of Fangio's or Ascari's, preventing him from attaining their level of consistency. It was also a style that took a lot out of the cars.

5. Mike Hawthorn

The 1958 World Champion - Britain's first - retired immediately he'd achieved the honour and died in a road crash just a few months later. Along with Moss, Peter Collins and Tony Brooks, Hawthorn was part of the cutting edge of British talent which rose to the forefront of international racing in the Fifties.

A wild, partying lifestyle off-track belied the commitment he applied behind the wheel. He was able to combine the two only thanks to a talent which, when it blew hot, was capable of greatness, the sort which enabled him to beat Fangio in a straight fight at Reims in 1953, his first season with a top-flight team.

But performances of such a calibre were relatively rare, and even though he was never anything other than a front runner, his exploits did not have the continuous thread of genius of, say, Moss. Perhaps this was partly due to his health; he suffered from a kidney illness which would probably have prevented him surviving much beyond his forties.

6. Tony Brooks

Quiet, unassuming and tending to stand in the shadow of Moss, with whom he was teamed at Vanwall, Brooks nonetheless had a beautifully natural, easy way with a race car. His lovely flowing style was seen to best effect on the sort of fast circuits which proliferated in the Fifties, such as Spa-Francorchamps and the Nurburgring.

Success came early. He was a dental student studying for his finals in 1955 when he won the Syracuse Grand Prix for Connaught at the age of 23. Stints at BRM, Vanwall and Ferrari saw him at his greatest and in 1959 his handling of the front-engined Ferrari in his efforts to stay in contention with the mid-engined onslaught, was awesome.

Deeply religious, Brooks came to consider motor racing with some conflict after a couple of serious accidents, feeling that it was morally wrong to take unnecessary risks. Although he continued to compete into the early Sixties, he was content to fade quietly out of racing thereafter, his true genius unappreciated by too many.

7. Giuseppe Farina

The inaugural World Champion, Farina's best years were lost to the war. Just prior to that he was one of the very fastest of his generation, though his approach was sometimes characterised by bravery over technique, slightly incongruous for a Doctor of Law.

Post-war he was included in Alfa-Romeo's squad but even in his title-winning year he was never quite a match for the speed of his team-mate Fangio. It was a similar story when he transferred across to Ferrari where he was teamed with Ascari. At times, however, his tactics bordered on the brutal. If any driver reflected what was to come in the Eighties and Nineties, it was Farina.

Right to end of his career he raced with a spirit and fight which could be formidable and on the odd occasion when Fangio or Ascari fell by the wayside, he seemed to be able to raise his game to the level seen briefly pre-war. It was only then that the racing world saw what it had lost.

He died in a road accident in 1966, a fate which Fangio, for one, always believed lay in store for him.

8. Peter Collins

Collins was a front-rank driver who is best remembered for surrendering his chances of the 1956 world championship to team-mate Fangio, 'because he deserved it.'

Collins spent much of his time driving alongside his great friend Hawthorn - 'Mon Ami Mate!' - and there was little to split them in effectiveness. Collins tended, perhaps, to be more consistent though Hawthorn was the one more likely to produce an inspired performance.

His chivalry in handing over his Ferrari to Fangio at Monza in 1956 made him one of the very few drivers Enzo Ferrari seemed to have a genuine affection for. It was all the more tragic, therefore, that he met his death in a Ferrari in the 1958 German Grand Prix, running off the road while trying to keep up with the Vanwall of Tony Brooks.

9. Jean Behra

The perennial underdog, Behra produced many against-the-odds performances during several seasons in a series of underpowered Gordinis and thereafter for Maserati and BRM. On several occasions he proved to have shattering pace, though his judgement in pacing a race often proved highly suspect.

A former motorcycle racer, he made his name in F2 with Gordini, beating Ascari's Ferrari to win the non-championship Reims Grand Prix in 1952. At Maserati he showed sparkling form in 1957 when he occasionally even ran ahead of team-mate Fangio. Some say he was desperately unlucky not to win that year's British Grand Prix, others that the failure

to do so was surely a result of taking too much out of the car in his desperation to stay in front. It was the sort of criticism which would continue to crop up, particularly during his short stint with Ferrari in 1959. He was eventually sacked mid-season at Reims after punching team manager Romolo Tavoni after an altercation.

He was killed just under two months later racing a Porsche at Avus in Germany.

10. Jack Brabham

Cooper's double World Champion, Brabham was the driver who broke all the rules. Rules which said that the driver never takes up a spanner or a welding torch - Jack did, and later went on to win another title in his own car. Rules which say that there is only one ideal line through a corner - Jack had several of them and they all seemed to work, even if he was uncouth enough often to shower following rivals with stones…

Raised on dirt-track racing in Australia, he took to the simple, rugged Coopers like a duck to water. He became the forerunner of the modern driver/technician, always keen to tinker, and in the cockpit he had an unerring eye for the killer punch.

It was a strong armoury, but on the other hand he was consistently overshadowed when pitted against drivers of real speed, whether it be Moss in the privateer Cooper or later on with Rindt and Ickx in his own Brabhams.

Mercedes and marketing

In the 40 years between Mercedes' withdrawal from F1 as a constructor and its return in the mid-nineties as an engine supplier, Grand Prix racing has changed fundamentally and grown exponentially. It left a Grand Prix world of which non-enthusiasts were only vaguely aware, where the factory teams were the major players, and the Grand Prix cars still had an engineering thematical thread with the road cars produced by those companies.

It returned in the nineties to the most intensely promoted sport in existence, the single biggest annual sporting contest on the planet. Less of a sport, in fact, more of a global marketing platform, not just for the car-related companies involved, but also commercial entities whose products or services are entirely divorced from the automotive world. For them, that the sport is a contest involving cars is incidental. It's the popularity and image which is essential. To an extent, this is true even of the car companies involved.

The car-producing factories no longer have their own teams; the specialisation necessary and the historical circumstance of the power base of the sport have seen to that. Instead they have partners, specialists who produce the cars - carbon-fibre, mid-engined projectiles with little recognisable technology from everyday cars - into which the factory engines are installed.

In an environment where the relationship between the products of these factories and the cars on the track is so apparently tenuous - in engineering terms and in the fact that they are merely a partner in the car - a company such as Mercedes clearly still perceives a substantial benefit. Mercedes marketing manager Michael Bock says: "It's all about supporting our brand image, one of dynamism."

Dynamism isn't a concept one would have automatically assigned to the products Mercedes just a few years ago. Fantastically solid engineering, yes, invariably crushingly capable in all areas too. Upper crust cars, but not really dynamic. "Mercedes has always had the core values of safety, quality, comfort and reliability," continues Bock, "but there are now new target groups - mainly younger ones - which means that we need to add other qualities to the traditional Mercedes ones."

What are these values? "Pleasure of driving, forms, colours, values which we understand as being hedonistic and which in the past have not been a strong part of the Mercedes brand," answers Bock. It's the image of F1, in other words - hedonistic, fast-moving, dynamic, colourful - which has attracted Mercedes to it this time around rather than any inferred technical superiority.

Yet, even though the reason for involvement may be primarily image-unrelated to the technical aspects of the cars, surely there will be a propaganda value if and when the cars do achieve a World Championship? Surely then is when the downside to having a partner comes into play - ie Mercedes will not be able to take all the credit. "Obviously it would be easier to communicate a pure Mercedes F1," allows Bock, "or at least it would take less action to communicate. But this is theoretical only because in modern F1 such an engagement - and we would have to do it without commercial sponsors - would not be financially realistic even for a major manufacturer. But in actuality having a partner like McLaren makes the marketing of the values we are trying to get across even easier."

The sheer size, scope and perceived values of modern F1 compared to the specialist interest endeavour it was in the fifties is reflected in the similar expansion of horizons for a company like Mercedes. Global markets and communications define this expansion; "You just can't compare the times," reflects Bock. "The company developed during those 40 years from a regional German car manufacturer to a true global player."

Personalities

Enzo Ferrari

Founder of the most revered of all racing teams, Enzo Ferrari was variously described during his lifetime as the most legendary figure in the history of the sport, an unpleasant autocrat, a misunderstood and basically kindly man, a crude Italian peasant, an organisational genius, a man who revelled in conflict, a caring father who never got over the death of his son, a manipulator of men. He was perhaps all of these in some measure, but the one thing he never was was unremarkable, and right to the end his devotion to the team he created was total.

The son of a metal worker, he had an early fascination with cars and motorcycles. After serving in the army in the First World War, he gained a job driving lorry chassis to the coachworks. With a dream of becoming a racing driver he frequented the cafe bars near Milan where many of the racing fraternity hung out, and befriended Ugo Sivocci, chief tester and sometime race driver for a company called CMN. Ferrari successfully persuaded Sivocci that he needed an assistant and, with an evident flair for making himself needed, he was soon gaining his first competition experiences in small-time events.

From there he gained for himself a similar role at Alfa-Romeo. Not, at the time, a particularly high-profile marque but one which had plans which involved racing. Ferrari would be tester and sometime racer. His skills as a driver proved little more than adequate, but victory in a small-time sports car event saw him presented with a shield bearing the prancing horse emblem of the late fighter ace Franco Baracca by the pilot's father. This was subsequently adopted by Ferrari as his personal badge of honour and remains on the cars which bear his name. His limitations as a driver were exposed when Alfa entered him in the French Grand Prix of 1924. After trying his car in practice, he appears to have feigned an illness and caught a train home. He ceased to have any significant prospects as a driver from that day and instead concentrated on running the Alfa dealerships he had acquired.

In 1929 he formed his own race team, Scuderia Ferrari, initially running an assortment of sports cars and motorbikes. His links with Alfa were still close though and when it decided to return to Grand Prix racing in an unofficial capacity in 1930, Scuderia Ferrari became the competition arm of the company in all but name. In partnership with drivers such as Tazio Nuvolari and Achille Varzi the team scored prolifically, but in the late Thirties Ferrari's long partnership with Alfa came to an abrupt end after he clashed with the new regime. The next move - the manufacture of his own race cars - was an obvious one and two sports cars from his workshops took part in the 1940 Millie Miglia.

When racing resumed after the war there were Grand Prix cars bearing the name Ferrari. There have been ever since. He remained at the head of the team until his death in 1988, an all-powerful patriarch with a self-cultivated air of mystique.

Tony Vandervell

A British industrialist passionate about motor racing, Tony Vandervell had a vision. He foresaw a day when a British Grand Prix car could take on and beat the previously all-conquering continentals. Forthright, determined and straight as a die, he was also vastly wealthy. It was a combination which created the marque of Vanwall, World Champion Constructor of 1958.

Born into a family of with substantial engineering interests, it was no great surprise when Guy Anthony Vandervell took up car and motorcycle racing in his youth in the Twenties. His involvement might have ended there as he took the helm of the family business, but for the development during wartime of the 'Clevite' thinwall bearing in America. Used extensively in aircraft engines, Vandervell's company acquired the sole European rights to its production.

It was a fantastically shrewd move and would earn Vandervell a vast fortune as its use became almost universal in both the aircraft and motor industry. It also transformed Ferrari's original anaemic slow-revving Colombo-designed V12 powerplant into a competitive unit.

Vandervell was one of the key figures approached by former racer Raymond Mays in setting up the BRM racing team. Mays' idea of creating a Grand Prix car built in Britain, funded by British industry appealed strongly to Vandervell who became a key board member of the fledgling company as well as a major investor.

It was not a match made in heaven. The straight-talking, uncomplicated Vandervell quickly became disenchanted with the top-heavy organisation and the horrific reliability problems suffered by the ludicrously over-complicated BRM V16. He decided to go it alone, answering to no-one but himself, the way he had always worked.

Initially he approached Alfa-Romeo about purchasing one of its Alfettas but was turned down flat. His next stop was Ferrari and here he had considerably more bargaining power. After Enzo Ferrari initially refused his request Vandervell had no qualms about threatening to halt Ferrari's supply of thinwall bearings. A Grand Prix Ferrari 125C was duly delivered to Vandervell's workshops in 1949.

When Vandervell inspected the car close up, he was less than impressed. Indeed he was furious, convinced Ferrari had sent him a cobbled together piece of junk. The Italian, used to dealing with fawning customers grateful for anything he would sell them, had underestimated Vandervell, a man who routinely negotiated with captains of industry. The replacement car was also sent back and it was Ferrari's third delivery, a 4.5 model, which finally satisfied Vandervell and became the Thinwall Special.

Enzo Ferrari by this time had become paranoid about Vandervell, convinced that this was all a ruse to supply technology to BRM, even though Vandervell had long-since severed his links with that company.It was probably with this in mind that Ferrari kept Vandervell waiting for three hours after an agreed appointment time at the Ferrari factory. Furious, Vandervell stormed out and returned resolved to build his own F1 machines that would 'beat those bloody red cars'. Thus the Vanwall line was initiated.

The achievement of his goal in 1958 was

Vandervell, Moss and Vanwall made a fearsome combination.

Clockwise, from bottom left: Raymond Mays; Tony Vandervell; Alfred Neubauer; Enzo Ferrari.

In the mid-Fifties Mercedes meant Silver Arrows, Fangio and… Neubauer.

clouded horribly by the death of one of his drivers, Stuart Lewis-Evans, in the final race of the season. Wracked with guilt that this could have happened in one of his cars, Vandervell had his vast enthusiasm for the project knocked out of him. The team would stumble on for a time, but it was never the same and when he then began to suffer ill health Vandervell called it a day. He died in 1967.

Alfred Neubauer

The legendary Mercedes team manager whose massive frame would characteristically be seen hanging out the pit signals to his 'Silver Arrows', Neubauer ran the team with a rod of iron. He is remembered, however, as a warm-hearted and highly amusing man by those who got to know him.

His association with Mercedes-Benz came about through his working relationship with Ferdinand Porsche; Neubauer had worked as a production engineer and test driver at Porsche's Austro-Daimler company, and occasionally competed. When Porsche joined Mercedes as a designer in 1923, Neubauer went with him. He again managed to get himself behind the wheel and was even a member of Mercedes' Grand Prix team at Monza in 1924.

Paralleling Enzo Ferrari at a similar stage in his career, he had limitations as a driver and his real talent lay in organisation. In 1926 he became Mercedes team manager and with a sharp as well as orderly brain, he soon had the team running with clockwork efficiency. He would direct operations with much flourishing and gesturing and devised a system of coloured flags with which to communicate with his drivers. He brought a science to the operation of running a team, typically Germanic in its thoroughness, but also characteristically unbending. There was the time when a car sprung a radiator leak in a race in Britain and rather than improvising, Neubauer had a specialist welder flown from Stuttgart; he completed his task in a few minutes and then returned home.

When Mercedes returned fulltime to Grand Prix racing with a Nazi-backed programme in the 750kg formula, Neubauer's talents came into their own. Grands Prix then lasted several hours and featured countless pit stops, and Mercedes would routinely make up whole chunks of time over the Auto Union and Alfa-Romeo teams in the pits.

There was, however, some suggestion

during this time that he was too much of a disciplinarian and that team morale suffered as a result. It also seems that he strongly favoured Mercedes' golden boy Rudolph Caracciola over the other team members, something which led to several screaming matches with the mercurial Luigi Fagioli. Yet always Neubauer's will was imposed. It should be remembered also that this was a time of racing for nationalist propaganda and that the directives for the nationality of the winning driver - Mercedes was often so far out ahead it could afford such a luxury of choice - came from higher up the chain of command than Neubauer.

'Moss remembers… the self-deprecating, rumbustious, big-eating, big-drinking bear of a man who would appear after the race'

When Mercedes returned to racing in the early Fifties Neubauer, now a full 20 stone, was again in the director's chair. He orchestrated a successful sports car programme before returning to Grand Prix in 1954, the team winning Fangio the World Championship at the first attempt. The following year the Argentinian was joined by Moss, who remembers not so much the iron-willed man in the pits as the self-deprecating, rumbustious, big-eating, big-drinking bear of a man who would appear after the race.

Raymond Mays

A highly successful driver in the Twenties and Thirties, Mays was also the man behind two racing marques, ERA and BRM. One was a pre-war endeavour and immediately successful in its limited aspirations. The other was post-war, incredibly ambitious and only successful after many years of tortured unrewarded toil.

Born into a comfortably-off wool business family, Mays was public school and Cambridge University educated and inherited his father's love of cars. Enlisting the help of schoolfriend Amherst Villiers he modified his roadgoing Hillman and enjoyed much success in hillclimbs and handicap events at Brooklands. The Hillman was then traded for a Brescia Bugatti and with this he reallybegan to make a reputation for himself, helped again by Villiers and also another engineering friend, Peter Berthon. For the

next 10 years these three worked on a variety of machinery , invariably raced with great success by Mays in British club racing.

But on an international stage Britain was going nowhere fast, not in Grands Prix, not even in voiturette racing (akin to Formula 2). Mays' development of a Riley hillclimb car in the early Thirties inspired his friend and fellow Brooklands competitor Humphrey Cook with an idea that would see a highly competitive British voiturette racer.

This was the birth of the ERA (English Racing Automobile). Mays, Cook and Berthon founded a company and set up workshops behind Mays' house in Bourne. The six cylinder supercharged Riley engine was used as the basis for the new car, a square-cut, upright single-seater. It was almost instantly successful, Mays' achievements with it against continental opposition giving the factory plenty of orders for replicas. The model formed the basis for British club racing through the remainder of the Thirties and some examples of the car racing in the historic classes today have an unbroken record of competition since that time.

Gratifying though this success was,Mays felt he had bigger fish to fry. He severed his connections with Cook and ERA on the eve of war, with the intention of building a Berthon-designed Grand Prix car in the former ERA premises. Obviously, the dream would have to wait, but during the war years Mays considered how he might fund such a venture while Berthon drew up plans for an incredibly complex 1.5 litre supercharged V16 car.

The funding solution was ingenious: Mays approached British industry with the idea of contributing to a flag-waving Grand Prix project that would advertise post-war Britain as a centre of engineering excellence. It was an inspirational idea, perfect for the times, and the donations came flooding in. BRM (British Racing Motors) was thus born. But if the idea was good, the concept of Berthon's car was deeply flawed. Although producing prodigious power it could never do so for very long and after literally years of embarrassing delays and on-track failures its time ran out.

Mays kept the faith and was there to see BRM take its maiden victory in 1959, 12 years after the BRM Trust was set up, and to see it take its only World Championship three years later. By this time Mays was more consultant than project leader, a role which he retained right to the last days of BRM in 1976. ●

Glorious failure: Mays' BRM V16.

BOSS
HUGO BOSS

The Top Five Races

Mark Hughes

It took good men to beat Fangio (far right, top). Hawthorn (inset above) managed it at Reims in 1953, while Gonzales (above) took third having turned the tables two years earlier at Silverstone, to take Ferrari's maiden victory (below).

Silverstone 1951

This was the day that the new vanquished the old, when the balance of power began to swing from pre-war carry-overs to a brave new world. Alfa-Romeo, its Alfetta design by then 15 years old, represented the past. Ferrari, in many ways Alfa's offspring, was the future.

It was a contest as rich with irony as poignancy. For Enzo Ferrari had been with Alfa at the conception stage of the Alfetta and his team, acting as Alfa's competition arm for a time, helped hone the car into the formidable racer his own cars now faced. Since the World Championship had begun 12 months earlier on this same Silverstone track, the supercharged Alfettas had won every single race.

For 1951 Ferrari had decided on a new tack. He took the option allowed by the formula of a 4.5 normally aspirated motor. It gave less power, but it sipped less fuel than the screaming Alfas. There had been some close calls earlier in the season but the Ferrari 375 just hadn't proved quite quick enough.

Silverstone suited it to the ground, however, and in practice Frolian Gonzales recorded the first 100 mph lap there. Even Fangio in the best of the Alfas was over a second slower. When the flag dropped it was Felice Bonetto's Alfa which screamed into the lead but he was soon demoted by both Gonzales and Fangio as these two made the lead battle their own. Fangio got ahead after 10 laps and over the next 15 laps built up a lead of around five seconds. But Gonzales was not unduly concerned; comfortably in second place, he knew the Alfa would need to take on more fuel than the Ferrari. Fangio tried every trick in the book to pull out sufficient lead for the stop but he was asking more than the Alfa could give. Gonzales even managed to repass him before the Alfa's stop on the 48th lap. As Fangio peeled in for his 49s fuel and tyre stop, Gonzales coolly eased his pace slightly but was still 36s ahead when Fangio rejoined. Over the next 13 laps Gonzales really got the hammer down and was a full minute and a half ahead of the Alfa when he called for his own planned splash 'n' dash, which occupied only 23secs. It just remained for him to reel off the remaining 29 laps and take an historic first victory for Ferrari.

Reims 1953

Although Grand Prix racing in 1953 was still dominated by the continental teams, that a 24 year-old Englishman had been signed to drive for Ferrari was an early signal of the winds of change. Mike Hawthorn's promotion to such lofty heights so early had been eased by the World Championship being run for F2 cars from 1952, giving him a stage to display his talents in an outclassed Cooper-Bristol.

Hawthorn was joining a team that was completely dominant, his new team-mate Alberto Ascari having won every single Grand Prix in 1952. It was the first time a British driver had stood a real chance of Grand Prix victory since Dick Seaman had been part of the pre-war Mercedes team. But there were a couple of obstacles he'd need to overcome first: one was Ascari himself, one of the fastest ever and at the height of his powers in an identical car. The other was the intensifying challenge of Maserati, led by the formidable pairing of Fangio and Gonzales. Hawthorn had played himself in gently in the first three races, taking a couple of fourths while Ascari blitzed another three straight wins. Then came the French Grand Prix at Reims.

Gonzales had opted to start on half tanks, hoping to pull out a sufficient lead to make a pit stop that the others wouldn't need, and consequently he leaped into the

lead. By half distance he was 20s ahead, but it wasn't to be enough. Behind him there was an almighty slipstreaming epic between Ascari, Villoresi, Farina, Marimon and Hawthorn. By the time Gonzales made his stop, this had been pared down to just Fangio and Hawthorn, now fighting for the lead.

Side-by-side the two cars would run down the long Reims straights, the two drivers signalling to each other and clearly enjoying every moment. Just out of the slipstream's reach, Gonzales and Ascari tried to join in but then became embroiled in trying to beat each other. Going into the last lap Hawthorn inched ahead and was still in front at Thillois, the critical final bend. He beat Fangio to the line by a second. Just 0.4s behind Fangio, Gonzales took third by a whisker from Ascari.

Aintree 1957: triumph for Moss...

Aintree 1957

Although Hawthorn's victory in France in 1953 had been a tremendous fillip to the stature of British motorsport, and had been boosted by the further successes of Moss and Collins, one thing was still missing. They had all scored their successes in foreign cars. Tony Brooks had taken his British Connaught to an impressive victory at Syracuse in 1955, but it was a non-championship event. By 1957 Brooks was now teamed up with Moss in the most serious Grand Prix contender yet to emerge from these shores, the Vanwall.

In the lead-up to the British Grand Prix, patriotic fervour was close to fever pitch. Brooks had taken second place at Monaco, Moss had started from the front row. Now at Aintree Moss had planted his Vanwall on pole. Could it all come together on race day?

The huge crowd that had gathered to find out saw Moss blast into an immediate lead from the Maserati of Jean Behra. Brooks, although he had qualified third

... disappointment for Fangio. ➡

Vanwall and victory

The first truly successful British F1 car and winner of the inaugural Constructors' World Championship, the Vanwall was responsible for turning the front of the grids from Italian red to British Racing Green.

After leaving the BRM organisation industrialist Tony Vandervell enjoyed some successes with a modified Ferrari known as the Thinwall Special. The ultimate aim, however, was always to create his own car and this eventually came about in 1954 with the first Vanwall.

Unsurprisingly this car had both BRM and Ferrari in its ancestry. When at BRM Vandervell had looked quite extensively at an alternative to the complicated V16, his idea being to produce a four-cylinder version of the Norton single which was dominating motorcycle racing in the early Fifties. This time he put the idea into action. Using one of Norton's original engineers as a consultant, Vandervell had the bike engine quadrupled up and combined it with a Rolls-Royce crankcase and crank, thereby using mechanical components whose strength and reliability was already well-proven. The chassis was essentially a Ferrari copy, albeit fitted with disc brakes.

Conceived originally for the two-litre F2 formula under which the World Championship ran in 1952 and '53, the car did not run until 1954, by which time it was under-engined for the new two and a half litre F1. Nonetheless, it showed some promise through the next couple of seasons, with American Harry Schell qualifying it seventh for the 1955 British GP. The car was by this time fitted with fuel injection which, like the disc brakes, was a feature adopted well in advance of either Ferrari or Maserati.

For 1956 the engine was finally given full two point five litre capacity and was installed in a new chassis designed by Colin Chapman. This was considerably more advanced. Chapman encouraged Vandervell to bring in aircraft aerodynamicist Frank Costin, who had already done great work on Chapman's Lotus sportscars. Costin produced a beautifully streamlined body for Chapman's chassis and the combination was sufficiently competitive for Schell to lead the Italian GP. All that was required for 1957 were some further Chapman changes to the suspension and greater depth in the driver line-up. To this end two of the best in the world, Stirling Moss and Tony Brooks, were signed together with the highly promising Stuart Lewis-Evans. The breakthrough came appropriately at that year's British GP at Aintree, where Moss and Brooks shared victory. There were a further two Moss wins before the year was out.

The same combination proved the fastest of all in 1958, Moss and Brooks winning three races apiece to give Vanwall that inaugural Constructors' World Championship. Despite the success, Moss remembers the car as being, 'quite difficult to drive, certainly not as easy as the Maserati 250F. The gearbox wasn't very nice and quite a lot of the time the engine had bad flat spots. But when they got it running properly the engine was quite good - though no more powerful than the Ferraris - but that bodywork made it very quick on the straights and the brakes were good too.

'Those qualities, the strength of Vandervell's determination and the driver squad that he gathered, were the reasons for the car's success.'

just 0.2s adrift of Moss, was still suffering from injuries he'd sustained at Le Mans in June and lay a circumspect sixth. After 21 laps it looked as though the dream was over as Moss' car slowed dramatically with a misfire. As Behra assumed a secure-looking lead Brooks was brought in to hand his car over to Moss. This left them down in ninth position but there were still

Though Behra fought hard (top) for Maserati, Moss and Brooks (above) would not be denied on home soil at Aintree.

another 69 laps to go and Moss was undoubtedly one of those few drivers who could pull off the seemingly impossible.

He rose to the challenge, passing car after car in a blur of lap records. At 60 laps, with Moss up to fifth, Maserati alerted Behra who responded by matching Stirling's times. Moss then passed Collins' Ferrari and, together with team-mate Lewis-Evans, began to attack Hawthorn in second place. But still Behra looked safe. Until lap 69, that is, when his transmission exploded. As Hawthorn came alongside he punctured a tyre on the debris. Suddenly Moss was in the lead! He and Brooks duly shared an historic win, the first for a British driving team in a British car at World Championship level.

Nurburgring 1957

The very next race on the calendar after the historic Vanwall win at Aintree saw one of the greatest individual performances of all time, one final magnificent retort from the old guard. The venue was the Nurburgring, 14 miles of 'green hell', the most demanding race circuit ever devised. The man who rose to the challenge of not only the track, but also the coming new wave of talent, was Juan Manuel Fangio, 46 years old and already a four-time World Champion.

The question concerning the teams before the race, held under a blazing sky,

was whether to run through non-stop or make a stop for fuel and tyres. Ferrari - with its team of Hawthorn, Collins and Musso - opted for the former tactic, Maserati - with Fangio and Behra - the latter. The Vanwalls, so effective at Aintree, were here crippled by their difficult behaviour over the bumps.

Fangio, starting on half tanks, reckoned the initial weight advantage - around 176 lb - would be sufficient to allow him to build up a lead over the Ferraris which he could retain after his planned stop. He didn't make the greatest of starts - Hawthorn led away from Collins - but was in the lead by the third lap and pulling steadily clear. He then began pulling out up to seven seconds a lap over the Ferraris and by the time of his stop on lap 12 was bang on schedule.

Maserati was not the best organised of teams and the stop took a hopelessly off-the-pace 53s, part of the problem being the need to fix a broken seat mounting. Hawthorn and Collins were 45s up the road by the time Fangio rejoined and there were 10 laps left. The pace of his first lap back out, while he bedded in the new tyres, was no quicker than the leaders and the Ferrari team breathed easy. But his subsequent laps were awe-inspiring; he broke and rebroke the record, lapping a full eight seconds quicker than his pole time in qualifying. By the time Ferrari realised the danger, Fangio was already in the leaders' mirrors and in due course they were picked off like cherries.

It was the Argentinian's 24th and final Grand Prix victory, and also his greatest.

Buenos Aires 1958

This was the race that signalled the final turnaround was imminent. From front-engined monsters to spidery rear-engined

minnows, from the reign of the factory teams to that of the 'kit car' specialists, from continental European rule to British.

Argentina was the opening round of the 1958 World Championship and because many teams had been experiencing trouble getting their cars to run on the new Avgas fuel demanded by the regulations, the entry was pretty thin. Vanwall was among the teams which didn't make it and so its contracted driver, Stirling Moss, accepted an offer to race Rob Walker's privately-entered Cooper.

Alongside the fire-breathing monsters on the grid the little car looked way out of its depth. Besides, Moss had qualified it only seventh quickest of the meagre 10-car entry, two seconds slower than Fangio's pole-sitting Maserati.

Fangio led away, with Moss fifth at the end of the first lap. But the further the race progressed, the better the little Cooper looked. Its light weight meant it was taking nothing like as much out of its tyres as the big Italian cars in the stifling heat. In fact so hot was it that everyone had elected to run a pit stop strategy, to replace the tyres and catch a drink. Everyone? Well, so Ferrari and Maserati assumed. Moss knew better. He was going to run non-stop. Apart from anything else, the Cooper's wheels were cast alloy and were attached by four separate wheel studs, whereas other teams used centre-locked knock-off wire wheels; a pit stop was not an option since it would have taken an age!

When Fangio peeled off for his stop, Moss took the lead. He never lost it again, despite a last-minute challenge from the Ferrari of Luigi Musso. The new era had begun.

Fangio's greatest drive came at the Nurburgring in that 1957 epic (below), but within months Moss showed in Argentina where the future lay (above).

Neck and neck: Olivier Gendebien's Ferrari just pips Bruce McLaren's
Cooper to the line for fourth place in the French GP at Reims, 1959.

A legacy of commonsense

Mark Hughes

Father and son Charles and John Cooper are credited with changing the face of Grand Prix racing forever. There had been mid-engined cars before - the Auto Unions had dominated in 1936 and won regularly over several seasons in the immediate pre-war period - but their competitiveness had been ascribed to their power, little more. Besides, they generally played second fiddle to the front-engined Mercedes of the time, and it required drivers of the calibre of Bernd Rosemeyer and Tavio Nuvolari to extract their ultimate performance. No, the Coopers' little creations generated such shockwaves because they were demonstrably more effective, even with a significant shortfall in engine power.

After Moss won in Argentina 1958, the way ahead was clear. Mid-engined layouts offered less weight, less frontal area and a lower 'polar moment of inertia' - simply expressed, the car changed direction more precisely. In 1959 mid-engined cars won every race bar one - and even that was a fix, an act of thuggery on behalf of the Italian Grand Prix organisers in a

successful attempt to give the front-engined Ferraris victory - and Cooper's Jack Brabham won five consecutive Grands Prix on his way to the world title.

But it was more, so much more, than just a change in the fashion dictating which end the engine went. Cooper taking over from legendary marques such as Ferrari, Maserati and, before them, Mercedes and Alfa-Romeo, was like a northern league football team winning the premiership... and then having more northern league teams join them there, pushing out the established superteams.

The Coopers were built in a garage in Surbiton and bolted together with components from here, there and everywhere. Coventry Climax engines, gearboxes adapted from a roadgoing Citroen, some Volkswagen suspension parts. It was almost a surprise that the cars were even built in a garage and not some corrugated iron lean-to! To some, those who believed that the purity of Grand Prix racing involved the finest car factories in the world producing a race car in its entirety, this was sacreligious. Nothing had ever been seen like it before.

And Britain? Grand Prix cars weren't made in Britain, not successful ones at any rate. Vanwall had only just taken the first fully British Grand Prix victory a few months before Moss won with the mighty atom in Argentina. At least the Vanwall was a proper Grand Prix car made in the grand manner, designed with input from the aeronautical industry, built entirely in-house and with its engine in the proper place. No, Cooper was nothing more than a jumped-up F3 team, surely?

Formula Junior, or Formula 3 as it subsequently became, took a real hold in early post-war Britain. Designed to enable the man in the street to get into racing, these tiny cars were powered by

500 cc motorcycle engines with chain drives. They were as basic as could possibly be imagined and were perfectly suited to the make-do improvisation mentality of a still-rationed Britain.

It should be remembered too, that this was the first time there had been a real opportunity for a circuit racing movement to take hold in Britain. For the first time, it had lots of circuits available, courtesy of all the disused wartime airfields. Pre-war there had been the odd road circuit, notably Donington Park, but generally the emphasis was on the concrete speedbowl of Brooklands, where the accent had always been on 'the right crowd and no crowding'. This type of racing was completely out of step with what was happening in continental Europe and the fact that Brooklands was rendered unusable after the war was, in hard reality, probably a further bonus for Britain's eventual standing in the world of international racing.

So Cooper represented a movement, but it was not one which anyone would ever have imagined taking over Grand Prix

So why was Cooper first to the post? Listening to John Cooper tell the story today, it's refreshingly, even hilariously, simple: 'Well with the chain-drive F3 cars it was a lot more convenient to have the engine at the back. We weren't looking at rear engines as some breakthrough in science. In fact we built the Cooper-Bristol F2 car in the early Fifties and that was a front-engined car. For practical reasons, having the engine at the back of the F3s was just the obvious place for it.

'It wasn't until we built the bob-tailed rear-engined Cooper sports car in the mid-

members of the public were killed when Pierre Levegh's Mercedes 300SLR crashed into the crowd, had its part to play. How so? This was the accident that prompted Mercedes' withdrawal from motor racing after just two years in F1. Of all the factory teams, it was the one with the outlook and resources to stay ahead of the game. A four-wheel-drive, V8-powered version of its already dominant W196 racer was on the drawing boards in 1955. Had such progress continued, perhaps the establishment would not have been so vulnerable when Cooper stuck its toe in the water of F1 in the late Fifties. Or perhaps Mercedes-Benz would have moved the goalposts too much.

That it was such a casual entity as Cooper which so embarrassed the grandees was almost a further punishment for the manufacturers' lack of vision. That it was such a team is evidenced by John Cooper's recollection from early 1960: 'Well, Bruce McLaren had won the first race for us out there, but Lotus was there with its first rear-engined car and it was very quick. I remember on the plane back

John Cooper (bottom, left) and Jack Brabham, unstoppable pioneers with the nimble green Coopers.

racing. The fact that it did essentially boils down to the fact that it employed the mid-engined layout at a time when the factory teams were being ridiculously conservative in not researching that route as a matter of course. The Maserati 250F in which Fangio won the World Championship in 1957 was inherently the same basic model which had debuted in '54 and which itself was really only a development of its F2 car of '52. The Ferraris were no more advanced either, once Maranello had erased much of the innovative enterprise of Vittorio Jano as it took over the Lancia D50s for 1956.

'with the chain-drive F3 cars it was a lot more convenient to have the engine at the back'

Fifties that we thought we might be on to something. That was a super car, very light, very easy on its tyres, you sat low down... and it was very cheap. It just seemed so right. Then we built a single-seater version of that and as soon as Climax built a twin-cam version of its engine instead of a single-cam, we had something that we could do something with. We'd entered Grands Prix before that, of course, but that was simply because the regulations allowed us to, and there was some start money in it, not because we thought we had a chance.

'Having said all that though, we were still, I think, as surprised as the other teams with that win in Argentina!'

So, circumstance, commonsense and natural evolution saw Cooper change the face of Grand Prix racing forever. The circumstance of a new grass roots circuit racing movement in Britain, the circumstance of that movement relying on motorcycle engines with chain drive, the circumstance of the factory teams not being sufficiently progressive in their outlook. It could even be argued that the Le Mans disaster of 1955, in which over 80

we were sitting - Bruce, Jack (Brabham) and myself - and Jack said, "Look, the only way we're going to beat them this year is if we go back and redesign the car." So, right there on the aeroplane, that's what we did. We designed a lower version of it, better suspension and better aerodynamics. It was just commonsense really.'

The success - and the relative ease of that success - of Cooper spawned a whole host of imitators, all of them from Britain where there was now a pool of motor racing knowledge and facilities, courtesy of the 500cc F3 racing. Lotus - which combined Cooper's kit car approach with more science - Lola, Brabham and McLaren were all in a very similar vein, the latter two even springing direct from Cooper's two works drivers by the Sixties. Cooper itself never recaptured the heyday of 1959/ '60 and in 1968 would leave the sport whose modern face it had created. And, just in case sceptics remain unconvinced of the influence of that 500 cc formula from which Cooper sprang, consider that it introduced to the world of motor racing one Bernard Charles Ecclestone...

Technologically
fertile

David Tremayne

There is a tendency for people to look back on the Sixties with rose-tinted spectacles, and in doing so to underestimate the decade.

As F1 progressed in the Eighties and Nineties, and its worldwide televisual appeal soared to stratospheric levels, some fell into the error of believing that nobody had ever attacked a corner with the commitment of Ayrton Senna, or driven a racing car with the fluid elegance of Alain Prost. But Stirling Moss and Jimmy Clark had possessed all of Senna's brilliance, perhaps more, and the same easy skill of Prost. Jochen Rindt had Senna's passion and fire. It was just that much less fuss was made about it all back then, for it had yet to become a media age, and motor racing was still essentially a sport. Back then Murray Walker was the wordsmith for televised races, but they were few and far between and were invariably broadcast in black and white on grainy screens that made identification of the cars a nightmare task.

The other crucial difference was that what media coverage there was - via weeklies such as *Autosport, Motoring News, Autocar* and *Motor* in the UK - and the national daily newspapers, all tended to centre on the sporting action. There was none of today's obsession with the minutae of the private lives of the stars at the centre of the stage. Back then they were, of course, famous, but the price of fame had yet to include any right to privacy. Despite the calibre of the drivers, the machines and the events tended to be more in the spotlight. The word hype had mercifully yet to be coined.

It was the Sixties, however, that would see some of the most profoundly influential changes in the sport's make-up, changes that would ultimately lead it down a new path to the territory that we recognise as F1 today.

The decade, like the Fifties, saw three F1 formulae. It began with the final year of the old, very successful, two and a half litre regulations, and 1960 was to prove the final hurrah for the front-engined racer. Rear-engined cars won eight of the nine races (discounting the Indianapolis 500

Ferrari's front-engined offerings were outdated as the decade began...

which was in its final year of a curious convention in which it had counted as a World Championship round). Even this was misleading for, already seeing plots everywhere via proposed new regulations limiting engines to one and a half litre capacity, the British contingent got a bee under its bonnets when it learned the Italian GP would be run round Monza's banked track and refused to participate. This bothered the tifosi not at all, and they cheered to the echo as Phil Hill's Ferrari won to record the last-ever victory for a car with its engine ahead of the driver.

'but for mechanical ill fortune, the Scot would have challenged Fangio's numerical mantle'

By 1961, when the one and a half litre formula came into effect, the only self-respecting cars which put their engines in such a position were either sports prototypes or Indianapolis roadsters. And even that would change all too soon…

Since Stirling Moss's breakthrough victory in Argentina with the little Cooper-Climax, the tide of British motor racing dominance had been turning, yet in what

now seems an unaccountable fit of dudgeon the British constructors came close to throwing it all away when the new formula came into being. They were doing very nicely, thank you, under the old regulations, and when the FIA mooted change as early as 1958 they dug their heels in and, ultimately, thrust their heads into the sand, convinced that the new regulations would not go ahead. When it became clear that they were indeed going to proceed, the British talked boldly of a rival 'Intercontinental' formula using the old cars or derivatives thereof. By the time they realised that the blind-eye approach was not going to work, Enzo Ferrari was laughing most of the way towards a championship that he must have despaired of ever winning while his front-engined cars were being thrashed by the new wave of British contenders.

By the time things settled down and everyone got on with the business of racing one and a half litre cars, it was far too late for the British contingent to do much about the powerful and beautiful shark-nose Ferraris, though Moss's brilliance put them in their place at Monaco and the Nurburgring. But even as Phil Hill won the championship crown that had been so sadly tarnished by the death of Wolfgang von Trips at Monza, the potent new British V8 engines from Coventry Climax and BRM were beginning to emerge from the test beds, and over the ensuing four years of one of the shortest-lived of all F1 formulae, these would prove the staples of the sport. By 1962 the British had picked up where they left off in 1960, as seamlessly as if Ferrari's front-running interlude had never happened. As the red cars slumped, so the little green Lotuses, BRMs, Brabhams and Coopers pushed back to the fore. Where, the world had come to realise, they belonged.

These were the innocent, carefree days of Jim Clark and Lotus when, but for mechanical ill fortune, the Scot would have challenged Fangio's numerical mantle with four straight World Championships. When two fellow Britons and an American would prove to be his only true rivals. And when Moss's accident at Goodwood in 1962, and his premature return, would see him involuntarily hand the baton on to the Flying Scot.

… but his sharknose cars redressed that a season later (below) before the British (such as Clark and Lotus, left) got their act together for the remainder of the one point five litre formula.

Clark and Chapman won more champagne than most (right), but South Africa in 1968 (above) would mark their last F1 success. The elegant Lotus 49 showed others the meaning of engineering excellence. Honda's 1966 offering (below) was one of many put to shame.

There is a tendency to see the little one and a half litre cars in retrospect as unworthy of F1 status, with their low power and their skinny tyres, but what made them great were the drivers who pushed them to the limits, and who cornered them far faster than anything that had come before. In many ways, underpowered or not, the 1961-1965 F1 was one of the very best.

There was, nevertheless, a widespread sigh of relief when the CSI announced that from 1966 the formula would cater for normally aspirated cars of three-litre capacity, while an additional paragraph allowed supercharged engines up to one and a half litres. This was all but ignored at the time, but as we would see in the Seventies, it was to have serious and far-reaching repercussions.

The years 1966 and 1967 were halcyon days for F1 in many ways, with a technical variety that has not been seen since. Over the course of this two-year period, before the great Cosworth DFV exerted its near stranglehold on the formula and forcibly distilled engineering thinking, there were myriad ideas on how to achieve the common goal of squeezing 150 bhp per litre out of a normally aspirated engine, and to win Grand Prix races. There were the superlight Brabham-Repco V8s; the peerless but fragile Lotus-Ford V8s; the cumbersome BRM H16s; Cooper-Maserati V12s; McLaren-Ford V8s and McLaren-Serenissima V8s; the clean McLaren-BRM V12; the gorgeous Eagle-Weslake V12; the hefty Honda and elegant Ferrari V12s, each with their spaghetti exhaust; sundry older formula Lotuses and BRMs with stretched two-litre Climax or BRM V8s. The engineering was frequently raw - looked at from a Nineties perspective, some of it was

downright appalling! - but no two cars looked the same even though many of them wore the same drab dark green. It was a grand time for enthusiasts.

Besides variety, the Sixties was also a wonderfully fertile decade for technical innovation. Four valve per cylinder technology gained a permanent foothold in this era; Colin Chapman ushered in a whole new era with the monocoque Lotus 25; the BRM P83 and the Lotus 49 revived the Lancia D50 concept of making the engine a stressed member from which the rear end of the car was suspended; four-wheel drive made a brief, if unsuccessful, appearance; transistorized ignition and fuel injection were de rigeur; there were general improvements in transmissions.

But the greatest changes embraced none of these things. One came in the field of aerodynamics. Jim Hall's Chaparral sportscars had been fitted with high-mounted aerofoils since 1965, when McLaren also tried them on its mobile single-seater testbed and, if you can believe it, forgot about a three second a lap improvement at Zandvoort. Various spoilers and add-on fins began to appear in 1967 on high-speed circuits

such as Spa or Monza, but then the aero-revolution really hit F1 like a hurricane in 1968. After the Belgian GP you were nobody if your car didn't have the tallest, most precariously mounted wing over its rear axle, or wide fins sprouting either side of the nose. The science was still very much in its infancy, but suddenly drivers were encountering a new phenomenon. Following too close behind another car could lose you your own frontal downforce, while the sort of catastrophic wing failure that befell Jack Oliver's Lotus 49B at Rouen that year, or the 49Bs of Graham Hill and Jochen Rindt at Montjuich Park the following season, were an indication that failure to keep such forces of nature in full harness could also have dire consequences. Many of the efforts were frankly comical, and nothing looks more ridiculous to Nineties eyes than a 1969 F1 car with stalk-mounted wings atop both the front and rear suspension. Mercifully nobody was killed by the failure of these silly appendages, and the CSI sensibly stunted their growth halfway through practice at Monaco. A variety of wings, half wings, tea trays and, in some cases, just bent bits of aluminium, then partly merged into the bodywork to circumvent the ban, and things settled down a little. It was all a very far cry from the fullscale wind tunnel era of the late Nineties, when the quest for aerodynamic perfection led to all cars bearing a superficial resemblance to one another.

At the same time tyre technology also advanced in leaps and bounds. The

decade had begun with engines developing around 160 bhp, and ended with the better three litre cars (those with the Cosworth DFV in the back) developing close to 440 bhp, and tyres had got wider and wider by the end of the decade to cope. They were still treaded, thought the smarter drivers were beginning to realise that as they became more worn the grip did not always deteriorate. By 1970 the first racing slicks would start to appear…

In many ways 1968 was the pivotal season of the Sixties. Before it ushered in aerodynamic wings, it also saw the innovative Colin Chapman stepping forward as the first team owner to take advantage of regulations which relaxed the ban on advertising on racing cars. Chapman knew all about sponsorship from his Indianapolis crusades, and now he warmly embraced the Imperial Tobacco company. At a red, white and gold stroke Gold Leaf Team Lotus was born, and it was the beginning of the end for British Racing Green. When Graham Hill delivered the

World Championship at the end of that fraught season it was the final endorsement that motor racing needed as a commercial medium. From now on the sport would no longer rely on financial support from the tyre and oil companies, as it had for decades. The corporate sky was now the limit.

There are some who contend that such commercialism would have been anathema to Jimmy Clark, but he was actually the first man to win in Gold Leaf colours when he took his Lotus 49T to victory in the Tasman race at Wigram in New Zealand. But the great champion had little time left, and his death in the Formula 2 race at Hockenheim on April 7 left the sport as devastated as it would be 26 years later after Imola. Clark was the king, the invincible, and his death left his rivals feeling small and vulnerable. The days of innocence died with him.

In the aftermath it was left to his pupil and friend Jackie Stewart to embark with even greater vigour on a safety crusade that was widely derided by those who believed that motor racing should still be a blood sport. Stewart, whose first World Championship would bring the curtain down on the Sixties, was not a man to shirk either risk or challenge, but he was smart enough to want both to be calculated. Just as the sport was reaching the stage where it was beginning to reward its successful proponents, so it was also coming to this realisation. But it was taking the vociferous Stewart to force its eyes open.

The decade that began with Moss's triumph at Monaco (below) ended with those ludicrous overhead wings (top).

The Top 10 Drivers

David Tremayne

1. Jim Clark

Jim Clark *was* the Sixties, and nothing summarised the middle years of the decade better than photographs of the Scot reclining in a green and yellow Lotus, dark blue helmet with its white peak cocked to one side as he set the car up for a corner.

There was something almost telepathic about Clark's relationship with Lotus boss Colin Chapman, a bond which transcended mere friendship. They were like kin, and they fed off one another. Each needed the other, though both would clearly have succeeded anyway had the relationship never gelled.

Clark had everything. Speed, courage, cool judgement and brilliant reflexes. And he was easy on his equipment. When he had to he could nurse it to the finish and it may be telling that he was the only man ever to coax BRM's H16 engine to victory.

They said he was at his best out front, dominating a race, and that he was weaker in the pack. But his drives at Nurburgring in 1962, Zandvoort in 1966 and Monza in 1967 showed that for the fallacy it was. From 1962 Clark was the best wherever he was - and all of his rivals knew it.

2. Stirling Moss

Stirling Moss was the man who could make the impossible possible, and time again he proved it. His innate talent allowed him to adjust seamlessly from the two and half litre era to the new one and a half litre cars, despite the lack of power, and his drives at Monaco and Nurburgring in 1961 were the stuff of legends and the equal of anything the other greats achieved.

With a better car in 1961 he would have walked the World Championship, and joint third place was derisory reward. Yet Moss made no complaint. He was at the peak of his form, the yardstick by which the rest were judged. It mattered not that he was in Rob Walker's private Lotus.

1961 was Clark's second learning year and there were signs that he would soon be challenging Moss's supremacy, but after Stirling's terrible accident at Goodwood in April 1962 the prospect of the two giants taking each other on was to be denied the sport, just as was a prolonged showdown between Senna and Schumacher. By his own admission Stirling came back too soon, and quit too early when he felt he had lost his edge. Who knows what he might have gone on to achieve had he not felt so obliged to get back into the cockpit so quickly?

3. Jackie Stewart

Like Clark with Moss, Jackie Stewart was ultimately denied the chance of measuring himself against Jimmy in competitive F1 equipment. Yet his performances against his fellow Scot in F2 suggested that some fabulous racing had been in prospect.

Stewart epitomised the late Sixties, embracing modern trends such as long Beatle-style hair, black corduroy cap and big dark glasses. He was a man of his time, and a man who moved with the times, and as sharp as they come. Moss made money from his racing, but Stewart was the first to see the rewards of the big commercial picture, the first to have his own fitness trainer, unafraid of the limelight of publicity.

On the track he had flair and speed allied to the same professional courtesy as Clark and Moss. And off it he was a fearless campaigner for increased safety. Never one to shy away from a battle, he did more than any other driver to bring about the high standards of safety that tend to be taken for granted in the Nineties. His work on behalf of the Grand Prix Mechanics' Charitable Trust has raised hundreds of thousands of pounds, and his own Stewart Grand Prix team has already begun to make an impression. Outgoing, personable and a terrific ambassador for motor racing, the sport can count itself exceptionally fortunate that he remains such an intrinsic part of it today.

4. Chris Amon

Thirty years on, it remains utterly inconceivable that Christopher Arthur Amon never won a World Championship Grand Prix. Time and again, particularly in 1968 and early 1969, the finger-biting New Zealander was set fair for the chequered flag, only for footling gremlins to bring his Ferrari to a halt.

He was, said Ferrari designer Mauro Forghieri, the only man who could come close to Clark. And his ability to detect minute changes in his car was a thing of legend. It caught out Firestone technician Bruce Harre on the occasion when he deliberately distracted him and sent him out again in a test with the same tyres fitted, only to have Amon pit at the end of the lap and ask politely if there was any chance they had forgotten to change them.

Amon was disorganised to the point of chaos, but like Clark he blossomed with a steering wheel in his hands. Then he became a sublime individual, capable of anything. Until the fates let him down again.

5. Dan Gurney

James Clark told Dan Gurney that he was the only man that his son Jim had really feared, and the driving of this lanky son of an opera singer was indeed of the highest class. But if Chris Amon won the Bad Luck Championship, Gurney was his closest challenger.

Like Amon, he had the knack of quitting a bad team just as it was about to come good. He left BRM for Porsche at the end of 1960, only for BRM to win the title in '62; just as Porsche was going well in '62, it pulled out; he quit Brabham in 1965 to set up his own Eagle

team, only for Brabham to win the next two championships.

Yet none of that soured Gurney, whose intense character at races so frequently gave way to that broad Californian grin. If he had any failing, it was that he just loved to fiddle too much with his machinery.

6. Graham Hill

Look at qualifying times in 1967, when Graham Hill was Jim Clark's team-mate at Lotus, and the Englishman with the bristly moustache and clipped accent stacks up pretty well. They said that he worked hard to be quick, but if that was really true then the effort was frequently worthwhile.

In the one and a half litre formula he was often the only man to offer Clark a challenge, and if there was ever a chance of victory, Hill could be guaranteed to be close enough to try and take advantage. His successes at Monte Carlo are part of the sport's fabric, but equally laudable were the way in which he led Lotus back from the abyss after Clark's death; and the relentless manner in which he recovered to race again after his leg-breaking accident at Watkins Glen in 1969.

7. Jochen Rindt

Had Jochen Rindt found himself a drive worthy of his talents sooner than his move to Lotus in 1969, he would undoubtedly have won more than one race in the Sixties.

When he burst on to the F2 scene at Crystal Palace in 1964 it was clear that he had all the speed he needed, but his F1 career stalled in a succession of poor cars, such as the works Cooper-Maserati in 1966 and '67. Yet he so nearly won in the wet at Spa in the first year of the three litre formula.

In F2 racing he was the king, capable of challenging and beating Clark and Stewart. That says it all.

8. John Surtees

The only man ever to win World Championships on two and four wheels, John Surtees had the courage of a lion and an engineer's ability to detect a car's shortcomings. But if he had an overriding problem, it was that he tended to become too bogged down on the technical and political sides of his projects, to the detriment of his pure driving. Had he raced two decades later, that would have been an advantage, but in the budget-straitened Sixties it frequently sapped his efforts.

When it came to racing, however, Surtees was a hard man to beat, as Brabham discovered at Monza in 1967. Rouen in '68 was another reminder of how hot the fires could burn.

9. Jacky Ickx

Jacky Ickx's performance in an F2 Matra at the German GP in 1967 was simply mesmerising, as he took the underpowered little car as high as fourth place among the F1s before it broke.

It was confirmation of his burgeoning status, and a year later he won his first GP, for Ferrari in the rain at Rouen. A year later still he beat Stewart fair and square at the Nurburgring, as clear an indication of talent as one could ask for.

10. Jack Brabham

When he turned 40, Jack Brabham went to the grid at Zandvoort in 1966 wearing a long false beard, before proceeding to win the Dutch GP.

It's easy to overlook that, like Clark and Graham Hill, he won two titles in the Sixties. The second of them, his third overall, made history as the only time a driver has won both world titles in a car of his own manufacture, and he deserved his place in the sun just for that.

Never one of the most outstanding drivers on the track, Black Jack could nevertheless mix it with anyone when the mood took him, as pole position in the opening race of 1969, in South Africa, and a fighting third in the last, in Mexico City, reminded his rivals.

The Cosworth DFV

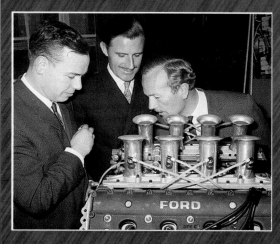

The three litre F1 was shaking down well by June, 1967. At the start 150bhp per litre was everyone's dream but few were anywhere close to realising it. Ferrari's V12 had perhaps 360 bhp, 30 more than the Repco V8. The Weslake V12 maybe reached 400, the Honda 390. Maserati's ageing V12 probably had no more than 350, while the horrifically complicated BRM H16 swam upstream with less power (around 380) than pounds.

The jury was still out when the Dutch GP rolled around on June 4, and then Keith Duckworth's Ford Cosworth DFV V8 simply redefined the whole thing at a stroke by winning first time out in the Lotus 49, and overnight rendered everything else virtually obsolete.

Ken Tyrrell, yet to enter F1 fulltime, astutely went to Zandvoort specifically to watch the DFV in action. He and Jackie Stewart were keen to work together again, but Ferrari was chasing the Scot particularly hard at that point. 'I told Cosworth to keep the telegram I sent immediately afterwards ordering three engines, when they told me they weren't selling any,' Ken said. 'Later I said to Walter Hayes at Ford: "You know, if we don't do something, this man is going off to Ferrari." Hayes agreed to underwrite the £20,000 salary that Stewart wanted from Tyrrell, and as a result the DFV went on sale.

'Without a doubt, I knew it was the future,' Eagle pilot Dan Gurney said after watching the DFV from the trackside. 'I felt with the Cosworth organisation and the hook-up with Ford and the modern manufacturing techniques - they were using tape-controlled milling machines - that this was a glimpse of it. The fan had been hit and it was the beginning of the end and the start of the future where the engine was the chassis. And from the sound it made, you knew it was gonna be making power. Though my heart maybe didn't sink, something else did. You could see it was a major change in technology. One of those historic days.'

'It just opened another door in motor racing,' Jackie Stewart, at that time struggling with the H16, said. 'It was immediately obvious that it was one of the serious considerations for the future. It was so simple, so small, it was completely obvious that the engine was something special. It looked like a Formula Two engine...'

Though so cammy that it felt to Clark like two different engines, the DFV produced 405 bhp in its original form and cost £7,500. And from 1968 onwards it enabled anyone with the drive and finance to build a good chassis to become an F1 constructor with a reasonable chance, at least in its early days, of winning races. It was the new Coventry Climax. It saw off all of its opposition until the advent of the turbocharged engines against which no normally aspirated units could hope to compete. In its various guises the Cosworth V8 was a pivotal factor in F1 from its debut in 1967 until its final victory in 1983. No engine has ever come close to its 155 victories.

Personalities

Colin Chapman

Like Enzo Ferrari, Colin Chapman was different things to different people. To drivers seeking a World Championship, he was the man who could make things happen, whose cars were fast and won races. To the faint-hearted, he was the man who made things as light as possible, and then fixed them if and when they broke. Some could live with that philosophy if it meant winning, others were not so sanguine.

Yet Anthony Colin Bruce Chapman was to the technological side of F1 in the Sixties what Jim Clark was to the driving. The Coopers came up with the first successful postwar rear-engined cars, but Chapman refined the concept further. His 18 looked like a modified eggbox, but from the 21 onwards Lotus F1 cars had an elegance all their own.

Jack Oliver's practice crash was the result of a cracked bell-housing, just for a laugh and to worry his rivals. Yet it was also Chapman who was shattered by Jim Clark's death. He was mercurial, exciting to be around, possessed of a brilliantly probing mind that could think laterally. He infuriated his men, but he also romanced them, coaxing better and better efforts out of them. Deep inside, they would do anything for 'the Old Man'.

And he left F1 a brilliant legacy. When Jackie Stewart was being courted by Ferrari in 1967, Ken Tyrrell warned Ford's Walter Hayes: 'You know, if we don't do something, this man is going off to Ferrari.' Hayes agreed to underwrite the £20,000 salary that Stewart wanted from Tyrrell, and only one problem remained. Hayes went to Chapman, who had enjoyed exclusive use of the new Ford DFV in its maiden 1967 season, and said: 'I think

Clockwise, from bottom left: Rob Walker; Louis Stanley; Colin Chapman.
Chapman's intuitive relationship with Jim Clark was a cornerstone of their massive success.

It was Chapman who introduced the monocoque chassis with the cigar-tube Lotus 25. Who pulled the package together so brilliantly and redefined the parameters with the ground-breaking 49. Who first experimented with aerodynamic wings in 1968, the year in which he was the first to embrace commercial sponsorship on the grand scale.

He was a genius, and as such he had his faults. He could be abrupt, at times downright awkward. Innes Ireland won him his first GP, at Watkins Glen in 1961, and never forgave him for sacking him almost immediately afterwards. Chapman did not even tell Innes to his face, but let him learn of it from third parties.

Chapman too, it was, who started the scare in the Rouen pit road in 1968 that

we're going to have to offer this engine for sale, don't you? Otherwise we're going to kill Formula One…'

And instead of screaming and ranting and guarding his own interests, Chapman had merely shrugged and replied equably: 'Yes, I suppose so.' He was, indeed, a giant in his sport.

Rob Walker

At the beginning of the Sixties private entrants abounded in the F1 ranks, the initial lack of a graduation formula such as F2 encouraging aspiring racers to plunge straight into the upper echelon.

By the end of the decade only the indefatigable Rob Walker remained, rubbing his hands with delight whenever

Jo 'Seppi' Siffert thrust the dark blue Lotus 49B with its white nose band towards the front of the field.

Born with the silver tumbler of the Walker scotch whisky dynasty to his lips, Rob was a man of the old school, raised to believe that manners were an integral part of one's make-up. His passport still lists his occupation as 'gentleman', and he has been one all his life, albeit an adventurous one. A lover of flying, he lost his licence for life after an impromptu display of low flying when he hopped hedges in his Tiger Moth and upset competitors in a point-to-point meeting.

When he should have been studying for his Finals, he chanced upon a three and a half litre Delahaye which he promptly entered in the Le Mans 24 hour sportscar endurance classic in 1939. He and his co-driver finished eighth. As ever, he presented an immaculate figure behind the wheel, wearing lounge suit and then changing for dinner.

When he married Betty Duncan, she made him promise to give up circuit racing, and gradually he turned to team management as a private entrant. During the Fifties he moved steadily up the racing ladder, until in 1958 came that remarkable moment in Argentina when Stirling Moss drove Rob's little dark blue Cooper-Climax to the triumph that sounded the death knell for the front-engined racer. Later that year Rob's car finished first again, when Maurice Trintignant won the Monaco GP.

It says everything for Rob Walker that when Tony Vandervell withdrew the Vanwall team at the end of 1958, Stirling chose to throw in his lot with the privateer team rather than accepting any of the offers he had to join other works outfits. The relationship yielded more victories, in Oporto and Monza in 1959, Monaco and Riverside in 1960, and Monaco and Nurburgring in 1961.

In March 1968 Walker's garage in Dorking burned out, together with his prized ex-Dick Seaman Delage and the remains of the Lotus 49 which Siffert had just crashed during practice for the Race of Champions. When Siffert then won the British GP that July in Walker's replacement Lotus, it was an emotional triumph, and the last time in which a true private entrant with a proprietary car would win the big prize.

Today Rob and Betty still travel to selected Grands Prix, Betty bringing her friends her homemade fudge for sustenance, Rob still able to dissolve a dinner table into helpless laughter with his string of glorious anecdotes delivered, as ever, in that luscious but unaffected drawl. Unquestionably, his passport description had it absolutely right.

Louis Stanley

Louis T. Stanley cut an imposing figure in the Sixties. Behind his back they called him 'Big Lou' or 'Lord Trumpington', and he himself did not always correct those who inaccurately addressed him as Sir Louis. He was tall and corpulent, with a ruddy face. His striding walk and blue blazer and pressed flannels, not to mention the old school tie, lent him an air of authority that few ever troubled to question. His presence was usually enough, when allied to his calm but authoritative and insistent manner, to overcome most argumentative protests before they had ever amounted to much.

His detractors - and there were many - rarely tackled him head-on, preferring to snigger behind his broad back, but even if he realised that he was being mocked it did not trouble him. Stanley had married into the wealthy Owen family which owned BRM. His wife Jean was the sister of industrialist Sir Alfred, who had rescued the ailing team and whose businesses pumped in so much money to finance it over the years. Stanley had two missions in

life: to see BRM again climb the heights it had ascended to win its World Championship success in 1962; and to do something about what he saw as the senseless waste of life occasioned by the lamentable safety standards in F1 in the Sixties.

He was one of the most outspoken and controversial figures in the paddock, and if his role as safety campaigner and senior statesman was somewhat self-styled, he was nevertheless prepared to stand up and be counted when it mattered.

Jackie Stewart's contribution to progress in safety has rightly been accorded due credit, as he took over from Grand Prix Drivers' Association president Jo Bonnier, but Stanley's contribution was also important and has tended to be overlooked. This was often due to his intransigent views on myriad subjects, which wrapped him in a persistent cloud of controversy. Like Jean-Marie Balestre, who would become the FIA president, Stanley's public image often did him few favours when it came to his actions being accorded their rightful recognition.

Medical facilities were frequently scandalous at circuits in the Sixties, and Stanley thus set about creating the International Grand Prix Medical Service, which comprised a fully mobile hospital unit which he launched, virtually single-handed, in the aftermath of the accident which befell BRM driver Stewart on the first lap of the 1966 Belgian GP. It was inaugurated at the Oulton Park Spring Cup in April 1967 when Lord Chesham handed over the keys to Director General Stanley, and the Bishop of Chester dedicated the unit. By the Seventies it had become redundant, eased out by politics, but Stanley had made the effort and the unit had saved lives. That was what counted.

After identifying Roger Williamson's body at Zandvoort in 1973, he wrote: 'Back at the Bouwes Hotel everyone was excited over a Championship victory, but that night and ever since I can see again the horror on the face of a young man who lay alone as others celebrated.'

Dogmatic and pompous he may have been, but Louis Stanley earned the right to speak his mind.

The case of the sailor's head

During the second session of official practice for the 1968 non-championship Race of Champions at Brands Hatch, Team Lotus chief Colin Chapman received a telephone call. It was from an irate ITV executive who informed him that if he didn't immediately cover up the sailor's head on the side of Graham Hill's Lotus 49, which was appearing in Europe for the first time since Chapman had agreed to paint the cars in the red, white and gold colours of Gold Leaf tobacco, all television coverage of the event would be cancelled immediately.

Prior to 1968 teams racing in Europe were effectively required to run their cars in traditional national colours - British Racing Green, Italian red, French blue, German silver. While sponsorship had always been a key element in American racing - back in the Twenties the colourful showman Barney Oldfield had his car plastered with indications that Firestone tyres were his only life insurance - in Europe it was looked down on and very strictly controlled. The tyre and oil companies, such as Dunlop and Esso, frequently provided funding to pay driver salaries, but they required

little identification in return and 'trade' sponsorship was condoned. Commercial entities such as finance companies Bowmaker and UDT had run teams bearing their own names early in the Sixties, but they did so without visible branding. There were rules that governed the size of any commercial sponsorship identification, and they were not generous.

In 1968, however, the RAC and the FIA bowed to increasing pressure from people who had to pay for their own motorsport, and were finding it increasingly onerous, and relaxed the rules on advertising on racing cars. At a stroke they opened the door to commercial sponsorship of motor racing. It was the beginning of the end of sport, and the birth of the commercialism that would be so rampant by the Eighties and Nineties.

Chapman's deal with Imperial Tobacco took effect in time for the Lady Wigram Trophy at Wigram on January 20, the third round of the New Zealand/Australia Tasman series. Clark started from pole, won the race, and added another three to wrap up the title in a successful campaign rendered all the more poignant by his death that April. But even then Chapman, and BRM, whose cars merely had their own patents pending stickers on the bodywork, fell foul of the Australian CAMS authority, which also objected to such blatant advertising.

That day at Brands Hatch it is worth pointing out that the unfortunate sailor's head was so small that you would have needed a magnifying glass to see it, while the black and white sets of the day made such things almost impossible to identify anyway. But that was the way things were then. The argument was that, while the colours of Gold Leaf were permissible, the sailor's head represented a brand identification which was strictly verboten. Chapman duly had the offending circle taped over and ITV went ahead with televising the event. Arguments over tobacco advertising, then, are really nothing new...

At the start of what would be a slipstreaming epic Jochen Rindt leads Jackie Stewart (20), Piers Courage (32), Denny Hulme (16) and Bruce McLaren (18) off the line in the 1969 Italian GP at Monza. Stewart and Rindt were closer still as they lunged for the flag 68 laps later!

The Top Five Races

David Tremayne

Monaco 1961

All thoughts of a dull formula were dispelled in the very first race to be held under the new one and a half litre regulations.

Ferrari began the season as the favourite, having bitten the bullet and prepared the elegant shark-nosed 156s with their flat 12 engines, as the British teams sniffed in the forlorn hope that the rules would not change. Yet in qualifying it was the Lotus 18 and the 21 of Stirling Moss and Jim Clark respectively that sandwiched Richie Ginther's Ferrari on the front row, with Graham Hill's BRM-Climax fourth alongside Phil Hill's Ferrari. All of the British cars were using the old Climax four cylinder as the new V8s was still a long way off being ready, but the tight nature of Monaco suited them well.

Ginther burst into the lead from Clark, but when the Scot's fuel pump began cutting out Moss soon swept through on to the Ferrari's tail. Then Moss, and Jo Bonnier in a Porsche, moved ahead on the 14th lap. Phil Hill had moved up to second place, 10s adrift of Moss, by the 30th lap.

By the 68th lap, however, Hill had halved Moss's lead even though the Ferrari's brakes were beginning to fade and its engine to misfire. But then Hill signalled Ginther by to attack again, and he slashed down to within a tenth of a second of Bruce McLaren's two and a half litre lap record of 1m 36.2s by lap 84. Moss equalled Ginther's time on the next lap, the pair of them lapping an incredible three seconds faster than they had in qualifying in the intensity of their fight! For the final 10 laps they were never more than five seconds apart, both right on the limit after two and three-quarters of an hour of racing. Moss, in the inferior car, finished just 3.6s ahead after 100 gruelling laps.

Von Trips, sharknose (top); no match for Moss on the 'Ring (below and top right).

Nurburgring 1961

If Monaco had been stunning, Moss's performance on the 14.1 mile Nurburgring, the greatest circuit ever built, was the stuff of pure legend.

In practice Phil Hill became the first man ever to lap the 'Ring in less than nine minutes, and was six and a half seconds faster than Moss, who was still driving Rob Walker's four cylinder Climax-engined Lotus 18, now updated to 21 specification.

A heavy rain shower just before the start made things unpredictable, but the track was drying as Jack Brabham accelerated his V8 Climax-powered Cooper into a momentary lead before almost spinning, dropping to third, regaining the lead and then going off for good.

Moss thus led Phil Hill for the first lap before the Ferrari sped by, but Stirling

Ginther scrambles into the lead at Monaco, from Clark and Moss.

regained the initiative almost immediately, and never lost it again. As von Trips came up to dice with Hill for second place in their World Championship battle, Moss made full use of his soft compound Dunlop Green-spot 'wet weather' tyres. Trips set a string of fastest laps but somehow Moss responded and maintained his amazing advantage.

Eventually the pressure began to pay off, however, as the Ferraris reduced Moss's lead to less than seven seconds, but just then a rain shower gave him a much-needed respite. As the rain increased, and

Hill survived a big moment that let Trips get away, Moss majestically increased his lead again and sped home to win by just over 21s, a fabulous performance in an outclassed car on the most demanding circuit in the championship and one achieved the hard way.

Monza 1967

In the Sixties Monza was one of the fastest circuits in F1. Devoid of the chicanes that would spoil it in the Seventies, it usually resulted in a slipstreaming epic as groups of cars 'towed' one another around. By sitting in the vacuum created immediately behind a fast-moving car, a driver with a less powerful car could save horsepower while being sucked along at similar speed. The art lay in getting a tow at the right time, and darting ahead when it mattered to claim a position.

The Lotus-Fords of Jim Clark and Graham Hill were the class of the field that year, though Dan Gurney's Eagle-Weslake was a strong threat on such a circuit. Clark took pole position from eponymous cars of Jack Brabham and Bruce McLaren, but after a confused start Gurney led. But after five laps Eagle blew up. Clark was already into his stride by then, but on lap 13 he suddenly swept into the pits with a slow rear puncture.

That left team-mate Hill to fight with Brabham and team-mate Denny Hulme, with John Surtees in a hastily built Honda which comprised a Lola chassis mated to the heavy Japanese V12, leading Chris Amon's Ferrari, McLaren and Jochen Rindt's Cooper.

Monza was set to be Clark's greatest triumph, until the fuel ran low.

Wings and things

In 1955 the Swiss engineer Michael May turned up for a sportscar race at the Nurburgring with a giant inverted wing mounted atop his Porsche. The Opel RAK 2 rocket car of the Twenties had also used such devices to generate negative lift, or downforce, but only May remembered that, and once people had stopped laughing about May's 'wing' they promptly forgot all about that, too. Had they but known it, they had just seen the future.

Ten years later the innovative Jim Hall put such wings on the back end of his Chaparral sportscars, yet though they were highly competitive nobody copied them. McLaren tried a low-mounted version on its Oldsmobile-engined test car late in 1965, yet despite a three second a lap improvement at Zandvoort, designer Robin Herd also forgot all about it. Even he can't believe that he did.

It was not until Monaco in May 1968 that the first indication came that F1 minds had finally begun to apply the same solution. Colin Chapman's wedge-shaped Lotus 49B had remained under covers in Spain, but in Monaco rivals took in its upswept tail and the small wings it had ground either side of its nose. Then, next time out at Spa in June, Chris Amon's Ferrari appeared wearing a relatively high-mounted wing over the rear suspension uprights, while the Brabhams had lower versions, too. Amon would have won the race, and said he liked the feel of the wing, though it was never as good when designer Mauro Forghieri moved it forward to the rear of the rollover hoop, thereby negating its effectiveness in Amon's view.

The performance of the cars was dictated largely by the amount of friction that could be generated between its tyres and the road, and the idea of the wings was to generate downforce to squash the tyres further into the road, thus complementing and enhancing whatever mechanical grip the suspension created. By the Canadian GP in September every one of the 20 cars on the grid wore an aerodynamic appendage of varying efficiency, though results were mixed. BRM, the last to fit one, claimed its wing provided 400 lb of downforce at 180 mph. Lotus claimed something similar for its rear wing, and 200 lb for the front fins. And this was just the start. By the ground effect era of the late Seventies, F1 cars would be generating more than their body weight in downforce.

After numerous failures of high-mounted wings, notably on the Lotuses of Hill and Rindt at Montjuich Park in 1969, the CSI banned them halfway through practice at Monaco, relenting sufficiently to allow them to be integrated into the bodywork.

The Spanish GP at Jarama in 1968 was probably the last F1 race in which none of the competing cars relied on anything other than mechanical grip and a smidgeon of downforce from the slope of its nosecone to keep it on the track. From Spa onwards, F1 was headed for the era of downforce. Once Pandora's Box had been opened, nothing would ever be the same again.

Hill opened up a comfortable lead as Brabham began to suffer a sticking throttle and Hulme dropped out with overheating. Clark had rejoined 15th, a lap down, but was flying.

Then, with nine laps of the 68-lap race to run, Hill's engine broke, leaving Brabham with a narrow lead over Surtees, who had shaken off his pursuers. But Clark was gaining rapidly and swept back into the lead on lap 61 after a stunning display. Then, going into the last lap, Brabham and Surtees surged ahead of Clark again as the Lotus slowed. Down to Parabolica Surtees forced Brabham to brake on cement dust which covered Gurney's oil on the inside line, and as Brabham ran wide Surtees sprinted to the inside on the exit to the corner and beat him to the line in a photo-finish. Two-tenths of a second officially separated them.

In the interests of saving weight Colin Chapman had gambled on a minimal fuel load for Clark. His brilliant chase had almost drained the tank and the system failed to pick up the remaining litres. It was one of the few times that Clark bit off his boss's head...

Nurburgring 1968

This was the race that should never have been started, for the Nurburgring was shrouded with mist and flooded with standing water as the 20-car grid surged into the unknown after an interminable delay on the line.

The weather in practice had been terrible too, a brief dry spell giving a slightly unusual look to the grid. The Ferraris of Jacky Ickx and Chris Amon were fastest from Jochen Rindt's Brabham, with Graham Hill's Lotus fourth from Vic

Stewart amid the fog, 'Ring '68.

Elford's Cooper. Jackie Stewart, who was not at all sure about the wisdom of racing, was only sixth. Urged to run by team owner Ken Tyrrell, Stewart used a set of hand-cut Dunlop tyres and knew he had to start well to cut down the inevitable spray. He emerged from the fog at the first corner in third place behind Hill and Amon, on their Firestones, but had taken the lead by the Karusell partway round the first 14.1 mile lap. Nobody saw him again, almost literally!

Driving with uncanny precision, and avoiding over-taxing the wrist he had injured earlier in the year, the Scot simply disappeared into the gloom to win by an incredible four minutes from Hill, who spun and stalled at one point. The ever-unlucky Amon retired when his differential failed, leaving Rindt to take third place, but on this day of days Jackie Stewart lived in a class of his own, regardless of the effectiveness of those Dunlops.

Monza 1969

In 1967 it had been Surtees and Brabham who sprinted to the line in the Italian GP. Two years on no fewer than four drivers would vie for victory in the last corner dash to the chequered flag.

Jackie Stewart travelled to Italy knowing that victory could clinch him his first world title with three races still to go. It had been a great year for the Scot and his Ken Tyrrell-entered Matra-Ford, for he had already won five of the seven races, though Jacky Ickx had just beaten him at the Nurburgring.

As he qualified third fastest, arch-rival Jochen Rindt put his Lotus on pole from Denny Hulme's McLaren, while Piers Courage's Brabham was fourth ahead of Bruce McLaren and Stewart's team-mate, Jean-Pierre Beltoise.

The race soon developed into the predicted slipstream thriller, and Tyrrell and Stewart had cleverly opted for a special fourth gear ratio which enable him to pop to the front on the laps when bonus money was paid to the leader! Initially there was a seven-car fight for the lead between Stewart, Rindt, Jo Siffert in Rob Walker's private Lotus, McLaren, Hulme, Courage and Beltoise. Then Graham Hill made it eight as he caught up in his Lotus. Then Hulme, Siffert and Hill all hit trouble and fell back, leaving Stewart, Rindt, Beltoise, Courage and McLaren to take turns leading as the race built up to its nail-biting climax.

Going into the Parabolica Curve on that final lap Beltoise nosed into the lead, but as Rindt battled with the Frenchman Stewart timed his run to the line to perfection, inching past them both. Rindt lost out by eight hundredths of a second, with Beltoise another nine hundredths further back and McLaren only another two hundredths behind the second Matra. Stewart's dramatic sixth triumph of the season duly clinched him his first crown in style.

Graham Hill, Colin Chapman and Jochen Rindt discuss slipstreaming tactics, Monza '69.

Racing through the murk of a race that would never be held today,
John Surtees in the Honda gives early chase to Jochen Rindt's
Brabham in the 1968 German GP at Nurburgring.

The milk and water man

David Tremayne

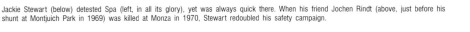

Jackie Stewart (below) detested Spa (left, in all its glory), yet was always quick there. When his friend Jochen Rindt (above, just before his shunt at Montjuich Park in 1969) was killed at Monza in 1970, Stewart redoubled his safety campaign.

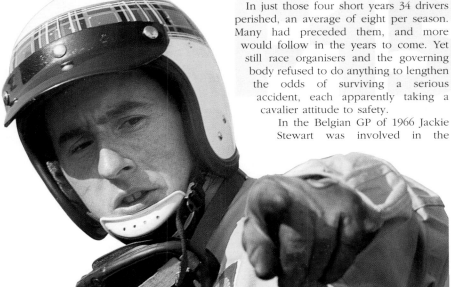

Jackie Stewart and his wife Helen once sat down and counted how many friends they had lost to motor racing, and stopped when they got beyond 50. Chilling and, to Nineties eyes, unacceptable statistics.

The Sixties was a dangerous decade in which to be a racing driver. Between 1966 and 1969 alone Bob Anderson; Lorenzo Bandini; Fehr Beat; Georges Berger; Jean-Claude Bernasconi; Lucien Bianchi; Luki Botha; Fred Brady; Oscar Cabalen; Tim Cash; Jim Clark; Georges Claude;

Paul Hawkins; Jose Jiminez; Erik de Keyn; Gunther 'Bobby' Klass; Chris Lambert; Wim Loos; Gerhard Mitter; Lee Oliver; Giuseppe Perdoni; Boley Pittard; Ian Raby; Doug Revson; Jean Rolland; Giacomo 'Geki' Russo; Lodovico Scarfiotti; Jo Schlesser; Mike Spence; John Taylor; Karl Thiemann; Roby Weber; Chris Williams and John Woolf all succumbed to motor racing accidents.

In just those four short years 34 drivers perished, an average of eight per season. Many had preceded them, and more would follow in the years to come. Yet still race organisers and the governing body refused to do anything to lengthen the odds of surviving a serious accident, each apparently taking a cavalier attitude to safety.

In the Belgian GP of 1966 Jackie Stewart was involved in the accident at Spa Francorchamps when a rainstorm hit part of the circuit moments before the field arrived on the opening lap, having just left a dry grid. Jo Bonnier, Mike Spence, Stewart, Bob Bondurant and Guy Ligier all went aquaplaning off the track on the ultra-fast Masta Straight. Stewart's BRM spun and dropped down a ditch, where he remained trapped in the slim monocoque of the damaged car, in fuel-soaked overalls, while team-mate Graham Hill and Bondurant worked desperately to unbolt the steering wheel so that the Scot could be released. The accident had a profound effect on Stewart.

'It was a terrifying situation, being trapped conscious in the car and being able to smell all the fuel around me. One spark was all it needed. When I was released, Graham and Bob took me into the cellar of a farmhouse and began stripping off my overalls, when a pair of nuns walked in. They were horrified by the sight they beheld, and it was a while before they could be persuaded to do anything…'

But it was a far from amusing incident at the time, and thereafter Stewart took over from Bonnier as the leading advocate of safety. By 1967 his BRM H16 was one of the first F1 cars to be fitted with safety belts. He always wore the best fireproof overalls, and together with Dan Gurney was among the very first to wear the Bell fullface helmets that began to appear in 1968.

It was not just the cars' and drivers' equipment, though. The circuits were manifestly failing to keep pace with the development of the machinery. In 1961 Richie Ginther set the fastest lap at Spa during the Belgian GP, at 131.530 mph; by 1968 John Surtees' Honda had upped that to 149.837 mph. Yet it was fundamentally the same circuit, with Armco guardrail in some places but open access to trees elsewhere.

Looking back from the Nineties, with the perspective of Ayrton Senna's death at Imola in 1994, it scarcely seems believable that Jim Clark's death on April 7 1968 should have excited so little progress. Perhaps that itself is a definition of progress.

Where the existing cars and circuits were changed within days of Senna's accident following a massive outcry, and the formula itself was revised within seven months, few lessons were learned when Clark succumbed at Hockenheim after his

F2 Lotus had suffered what appears to have been an explosive tyre failure and slid broadside into the trees.

In the aftermath of the Senna accident chicanes sprang up everywhere, and there was almost a drivers' strike in Spain until a tyre chicane was installed on a fast corner.

But nothing epitomises the distance the sport had to travel in 1968 than the situation which Stewart encountered in the middle of the season. This was not in some ill-funded overseas venue struggling to make ends meet or devoid of understanding of the sport. To their eternal shame, the organisers of the British GP at Brands Hatch, the RAC, behaved appallingly. It was as if they had barely noticed that Clark, arguably the greatest driver of them all, had been killed only three months earlier.

'We had been in correspondence with the organisers early in the year,' Stewart recalled, 'but their response could only be described as childish. We thought that a wooded area was potentially dangerous, and asked for a fence to be erected. It wasn't just something we were thinking of for ourselves, but for any driver in any race on what was a very busy circuit. Everyone racing at Brands Hatch would benefit.

'The RAC told us they didn't think that this was necessary because they were only "small" trees. Any larger ones could be protected by straw bales. Well, we'd seen what straw bales did for poor Bandini at Monaco…

'When we pressed the RAC harder we were told that if we wanted a fence, then we could have one if we paid for it! And they didn't even own the circuit, so it wasn't as if they had to pay for it themselves!'

At other times he was advised that if he wanted to have trees removed, the drivers could do it themselves.

Stewart's relationship with his entrant, Ken Tyrrell, was one of the greatest in history, yielding 25 GP victories and three World Championship titles. One of the few times they came close to falling out was at the Nurburgring that year, when the German GP was run in dense fog and on a circuit awash with standing water. Stewart did not want to go out to try out the conditions on raceday morning, and that gave rise to the only time that Tyrrell ever forced a driver to obey him.

'I said that I thought it was unsafe, it was just too much,' Stewart says today. 'The fog was ridiculous and the rain was really heavy. You know, I never did a lap of the Nurburgring that I didn't have to do. I

'The RAC told us they didn't think that this was necessary because they were only "small" trees'

found that out fairly early in my career. I defy anyone to say they really liked it, if they went properly quick there. It wasn't one of those things you went out to do a warm-up on. You did your warming up on the South Loop and then you went out on the big circuit and nailed it. To do the north circuit quietly was something I don't think I ever did in a racing car.

'So to go out there for that morning warm-up in the fog and with the water so bad, I was frightened that we would damage the car. And Ken said: "No, you've got to go out so you'll know where the water is." And he was absolutely right, there was nothing wrong in what he said. But I just thought if I damaged the car... I say Ken made me do it, but I suppose he really just convinced me it was the right thing to do.'

That was the key to Stewart. He was berated by some members of the media, who called him a "milk and water" driver. Whatever that meant, it was intended to be derogatory, as if somehow he lacked the courage of forebears who were prepared to take any risk in the pursuit of victory even if it meant paying the ultimate price. But Stewart was part of the new breed of drivers, not afraid of risk provided it was sensibly calculated. Yes, he led the lobby that ultimately killed the old Spa Francorchamps (a circuit that had itself killed some good drivers), just as Niki Lauda would kill off the old Nurburgring as an F1 venue more than 10 years later. But that day on the 'Ring in 1968 Stewart went out to race, and he won by four minutes. Not four seconds, but four minutes. 4m 03.2s, to be exact. It was the largest margin of victory since Stirling Moss had beaten Mike Hawthorn by 5m 12.8s at Oporto 10 years earlier.

At Spa in 1968 only a stop for fuel lost him the race. Next time the F1 cars went there, in 1970, the milk and water man was on pole position. There was a name for what he did: professionalism. Constantly he lobbied for greater awareness of safety issues - from driver clothing to car and circuit design and fire fighting; but always he gave his best in the car. Nor was this mere selfishness; he was concerned about the safety of other drivers and the spectators, too.

The more successful and famous he became and the more people would listen to his voice, the more he was prepared to use it until commonsense prevailed. If it meant the demise of the old Spa, so be it. And if others chose to criticise him for it, so be that, too. Stewart was prepared to put his reputation where his mouth was, on and off the track. It was a tough campaign, but he stuck to his guns. One man could not bring about a complete revolution. But without the safety crusade fought by John Young Stewart in the Sixties there are survivors of hair-raising accidents around today who would otherwise most certainly not have made old bones.

Stewart revered fellow Scot Jim Clark (far left). Following his death, and the lack of sensible barriers (left, Monaco) he dedicated himself to enhancing safety. But his concerns never stopped him performing brilliantly, as he did at Nurburgring in 1968 (below).

Driving all four wheels

In the late Sixties designers pursued two avenues to improve grip and thus cornering speeds: aerodynamic wings, and four-wheel drive. Where wings became an integral part of the F1 package, however, driving all four wheels proved a lamentable failure.

Ferguson was the first to try four-wheel drive, on its experimental P99 test vehicle which appeared in 1961 and, rather surprisingly, had its Climax engine mounted ahead of the driver. The system, which in modified form would appear on the Jensen FF roadcars, worked well enough to give Stirling Moss victory in the wet non-championship Gold Cup race at Oulton Park that September. Development for racing did not continue until BRM experimented with its all-wheel drive P67 in 1964, but Richard Attwood was withdrawn from the British GP. The system may have been deemed unsuitable for circuit racing, but Peter Westbury subsequently enjoyed success with a two litre version of the car in hillclimbing.

By 1969, when F1 cars were moving closer to the goal of 150 bhp per litre, four-wheel drive again became the buzz, partly because of the speed of the turbine-powered Lotus 56 and the piston-engined Lola T152 at Indianapolis and other USAC road racing venues. Lotus, Matra, McLaren and Cosworth all began working on projects.

Where the Matra MS84 was a slightly modified version of the two-wheel drive MS80 with which Jackie Stewart would win that year's World Championship, Lotus opted for the all-new 63, as did McLaren with its M9A. The Lotus and the Matra appeared at the Dutch GP in June, the McLaren at Silverstone in July. All were quickly abandoned by the respective teams' lead drivers.

It quickly became apparent that the inherent weight penalty was not going to be balanced out by superior traction for cornering, and Lotus in particular soon began to change the torque split between the front and rear differentials from its initial 40/60 ratio to something much closer to 20/80, which rather defeated the object of four-wheel drive. Jochen Rindt hated the car and usually left it to Lotus number three John Miles, but on the one occasion when Colin Chapman forced him to drive it he finished an uncompetitive second in the non-championship Gold Cup race at Oulton Park.

Johnny Servoz-Gavin drove the Matra to sixth place in Canada, the only time a four-wheel drive car ever scored a point, while the McLaren was quietly pushed away and forgotten after Derek Bell was saddled with racing it in the British GP. It was, he said, 'a right royal handful.' As for the brutally ugly Cosworth test car, company representatives would later wonder how on earth they had ever got so side-tracked.

In the end four-wheel drive failed because it was under-developed, the existing tyres did not suit it, and they were also doing a sufficiently good job on the two-wheel drive cars. And as aerodynamics became ever more efficient, so all-wheel drive was left to moulder on the shelf, another of F1's blind alleys better suited to roadcars.

The Multi-Coloured Circus

Mike Doodson

The story of Grand Prix racing in the Seventies starts with a one-time motorcycle dealer and gambler named Bernie Ecclestone. His rise to prominence started on two fronts. In 1971 Ecclestone became a team owner when he bought the Brabham team for £100,000. Soon afterwards, in a move which seemed much less significant at the time, the Londoner assumed control of the Formula One Constructors' Association (FOCA), the fledgling organisation which the British F1 teams had set up to negotiate their entries with race organisers. Brabham was to be a drain on the Ecclestone resources until one of his drivers (Nelson Piquet) at last won a World Championship in 1981. As we now know, though, he was also building up FOCA into a personal empire that would eventually make him Britain's best paid company executive.

Before the creation of FOCA in the Sixties, the advantage in negotiations with the teams had been in the hands of the circuit owners. Not only did they directly control the income of the teams but they were also the political force inside the Commision Sportif Internationale (CSI), the sporting sub commission of the Federation Internationale de l'Automobile (FIA) which would later be renamed Federation Internationale du Sport Automobile (FISA). Ecclestone broke the power of the circuit owners by unifying F1 under one command and creating a package which the circuits could take or leave, as they wished. His achievement was to make them want to organise races, even on his terms. The teams, which had never had anyone to represent them before, found themselves in demand.

Ecclestone ensured that the races took place (he regularly doubled as a promoter), gathered together the income and distributed it to the teams. All they had to do was to provide the cars and drivers.

Ecclestone's success was not exclusively financial. The concept of a World Championship which delivered one man as the winner at the end of the season had a brilliant simplicity which he appreciated and nurtured. When the FIA had instigated the championship in 1950, it consisted of six European races to which the Indy '500' was added purely for cosmetic reasons to justify the otherwise spurious 'world' description. Ecclestone was determined to conserve the image of the championship as the pinnacle of success, untouched by scandal or controversy. Although there have been a few grumbles over the years, nobody has yet seen fit to challenge an FIA World Champion's right to his title.

Public interest in the World Championship has never stopped growing since Ecclestone's stewardship began in 1972. It has converted F1 from a minority interest into a passion which preoccupies a world which is still taking the automobile to its heart. For the ever-increasing audience for the sport on television, the championship was an easily understood competition spread over a dozen or more rounds. Very soon it had overtaken other sporting disciplines which did not have the same control over their events. How much stronger would tennis or golf be now if they had been promoted over a unified series of events to establish an undisputed World Champion?

> 'Ecclestone was determined to conserve the image of the championship as the pinnacle of success'

Ecclestone's grip on the sport as the head of FOCA owed everything to his reputation as an honest broker whose member teams trusted him implicitly to get the best deal for them. He would not hesitate to put FOCA affairs ahead of the interests of Brabham, and often he was the saviour of a struggling team calling on him for a discreet loan. You would never describe Ecclestone as transparent, but he was always true to his promises. An impeccable judge of character with a network of reliable informers, he remained confidently ahead of the game. If he had a fault, it was a reluctance to delegate. But when you're doing business with someone, how much more direct would you like to be than to know that the voice answering the telephone is the man you want to talk to right now?

The tension that would culminate in the FISA/FOCA war of 1980/'81 was generated by the worries of Jean-Marie Balestre, the bombastic Frenchman who became President of the CSI in 1979. Suffice it to say that after an arcane battle over the ownership of the television rights to the FIA's championships, ending (at least in theory) with victory for Balestre, it was to Ecclestone that the Federation turned to administer those rights. His franchise with the Federation would turn him into a multi-millionaire.

The Seventies brought Stewart two more championships (above), saw sponsorship develop further (Alan Jones's Shadow, left, wins in Austria, 1977) and bred increasing confrontation between Jean-Marie Balestre and Bernie Ecclestone (left and right respectively, below).

Throughout the Seventies, most of the familiar physical landmarks of Grand Prix racing stayed comfortably the same as they had always been. Safety became more of a preoccupation, with the FIA setting down minimum requirements for crash standards and the use of safety barriers, which went through many stages of development. Nevertheless, it was reassuring that familiar venues such as Monaco and Monza survived with most of their character and tradition intact.

Not every temple of speed survived. A major rebuild in 1971 had not been enough to save the Nurburgring after Niki Lauda's fiery crash in 1976, and the hair-raising pre-war road circuit at Spa Francorchamps lost its race after the 1970 GP there. It would be eight years before Spa was upgraded, shortened and made safe for F1 cars again.

The most significant change was the international expansion of F1 in South America (Argentina was back, soon to be joined by Brazil) and in the USA, which by 1979 was hosting two World Championship races. The only setback occurred in Japan, where a fatal accident (two spectators in a forbidden area were killed during the race) was just one of the reasons why the Fuji Speedway said farewell to F1 in 1977, its second year as a host to the World Championship.

By the standards of the Nineties, the turnover among the teams was modest. March had been and gone, later to return in other guises, and for several years Matra invested hundreds of millions of francs without much to show for it. BRM, so often the sickliest of the British teams, enjoyed a brief period in the limelight before the candle guttered out in 1977. Tyrrell would never be as strong again as it had been in the Jackie Stewart era that ended with his retirement in 1973. But ready to step in was Frank Williams, who had conspicuously failed to achieve anything much for six years. A flirtation with bankruptcy got his attention, forcing him to start all over again: by 1979 he had found the knack and was on his way to the big time. Meanwhile, the names that appeared most frequently at the top of the results sheets were still Ferrari, Lotus, Brabham and McLaren.

When the decade began, Grand Prix racing was still coming out of a slump. Car manufacturers interested in racing had tended to put their money into sports cars and especially Le Mans, which sometimes attracted as many spectators in 24 hours as all the GPs put together. It was the ready availability of the Ford DFV engine, introduced in 1967, which gave the teams a reliable, sensibly-priced power plant. They could concentrate on building a competitive chassis without having to devote the energy and finance necessary to make engines. Although Coventry-Climax had done a similar job for British motor racing by supplying Lotus and Brabham in the Sixties, the DFV, built by Cosworth Engineering in Northampton, was available to any team which could afford it. At the original price of £7500 per unit, that included almost everyone. In 1974, the only F1 teams not using the British V8 were Ferrari and BRM. The sound of a V8 may have been a little too monotonous for some spectators, but the racing was close and the cars usually reliable.

These factors, coupled with the increase in television audiences, would be a magnet for sponsors, especially those outside the car industry. While Lotus had had Gold Leaf since 1968, a much bigger figure from the tobacco world arrived in 1972 when Marlboro sponsored a grandiose five-car team of BRMs proposed by Louis Stanley. Later, the French tobacco monopoly (SEITA) supported Guy Ligier with its Gitanes brand when the Frenchman entered the arena in 1976. As the outlets for cigarette advertising were closed by governments, so the tide of tobacco money increased.

While tobacco sponsorship meant big money and bold livery, the concept of sponsorship as a worthwhile business expense was being expanded. The first motorhome to be seen in the paddock was a John Player innovation, in 1971, and very soon the area behind the garages at European venues was occupied by an ever expanding gathering of American RVs offering shade, drink and food to the guests of that new breed of racing personnel known as the marketing man. Secondary sponsorships, often represented by only a comparatively small area on the car itself, added to the budgets. In 1970 Team Lotus had operated on less than half a million pounds: by 1979, that was the sort of money which a top six driver could command for himself alone.

Ford had been on the F1 scene since 1967. With the television viewing figures swelling, it was inevitable that the manufacturers of passenger cars should become interested in using GP racing to

Monaco (top, right) remained unchanged despite the growing tobacco influence, but Renault's turbocars (below and inset) would revolutionise F1.

sell their products. Alfa Romeo had been involved with March during 1971, using an underpowered V8. Starting in 1976, the Milanese company supplied Brabham with powerful but overweight flat-12s which kept down Ecclestone's engine bills but didn't win anything until 1978.

The biggest impact to be made by a car manufacturer would come in 1977 from Renault, the giant car group which was still nationalised at the time. In the mid-Seventies Renault was gingering up its image by fitting turbos to several of the otherwise bland models in its product range. The company was already involved in a Le Mans programme with a turbo-engined sports car when it made its return to Grand Prix racing (after a 71 year break) at Silverstone in 1977.

Had Renault known what would be required to win races with the turbo, it is unlikely that it would have tried. Nobody dared estimate the cost of the programme: one British team owner remarked wryly that the Regie's cost accountants probably didn't want to know! Once under way, the sophistication of the engineering involved in making a winner of the turbo stimulated technology on a scale which made F1 success attractive to other manufacturers. Anxious to follow Renault, BMW, Porsche and Honda would all follow in the early Eighties.

Meanwhile, the potential of Renault's turbo V6s had the British teams seriously concerned. If the French ever succeeded in getting the turbo to the end of a race, the hegemony of the DFV would, it seemed, be finished. It took the genius of Colin Chapman and his discovery of ground effect in 1978 to make cars which compensated for their lack of power with the grip which the new aerodynamic technology could confer. Simpler and less expensive than the turbo, ground effect won half a dozen races for Lotus before Renault had its first success in July 1979.

It should have been easy to see that the combination of turbo power and ground effects was creating a generation of racing cars which were much too fast for the circuits of the period. As engine outputs headed towards 1200 bhp and cornering forces lurched up to 2 and 3g, the drivers began to be seriously concerned for their safety. The FIA's attempts to curb the excesses were invariably nullified by the brilliance of the engineers. It was luck, not good management, which saved the sport from several possible fatalities.

The Seventies, however, had already been stamped as the decade in which Britain lost a generation of upcoming drivers who, with James Hunt and John Watson, would have spearheaded the new national wave. Safety and marshalling standards were panned after Roger Williamson died needlessly in his upturned March at Zandvoort in 1973, the victim of fire as fellow racer David Purley tried vainly to rescue him single-handed. The tragedy in which the ever-popular Graham

Hill perished late in 1975 as he crashed his Piper Aztec short of Elstree aerodrome in foggy conditions, took the lives of many of his burgeoning team, among them the brilliant Tony Brise. Welshman Tom Pryce was the innocent victim of freak circumstance and over-zealous marshalling at Kyalami in 1977. All had been potential champions, as had Francois Cevert, who died at Watkins Glen in 1973 just as he was being groomed to take over Jackie Stewart's mantle at Tyrrell.

With Stewart retiring, the Seventies said goodbye to Hill too, and other luminaries such as Bruce McLaren, Jochen Rindt (the sport's only posthumous World Champion), Piers Courage, Pedro Rodriguez, Jo Siffert, Ignazio Giunti, Jo Bonnier, Peter Revson and Mark Donohue.

Although the decade was set to end on a positive note, there were warning signs from Paris. Ecclestone's success, and his virtual ownership of the racing business from Grand Prix promotion to television, was about to be challenged.

His success in fighting that challenge, and in emerging from it with increased powers and responsibility, would come in 1981. But it was a sign that that man who had generated so much wealth for himself and others would be allowed to continue doing so.

The Ecclestone era was only just beginning.

The Top 10 Drivers

Mike Doodson

1. Jackie Stewart

Any argument about who was the best racing driver of the Seventies has to start with Jackie Stewart and Niki Lauda. Both men have three world titles, both are still with us. Indeed, survival was an enviable achievement in an era of flimsy cars and circuits whose safety standards were set by their owners. The two are also survivors insofar as they are still making a living (Lauda's the more handsome, one suspects) on the back of what are now rather ancient sporting reputations.

The F1 careers of Stewart and Lauda overlapped by one season (1973), yet they span the period during which racing drivers stopped having to grub

around for expenses and started buying private jets. In 1969 Stewart thought he was doing well when he picked up 25 per cent of the £80,000 in sponsorship which Dunlop had agreed to pay Ken Tyrrell. Only eight years later, Lauda persuaded Marlboro chief John Hogan to make him the sport's first dollar millionaire.

Since he walked away from his Tyrrell in October 1973, Stewart's achievements as an ex-driver have tended to swamp the memories of his extraordinary skills behind the wheel. A somewhat sickly youth whose father ran a small garage, he had the happy knack of persuading wealthier men to let him drive their cars. Self-discipline and assiduous physical preparation were two important strengths.

For a while Stewart languished in the shadow of his fellow Scot Jim Clark, who was only three years older. But nothing would prevent him from becoming the fastest and most consistent driver of the post-Clark era. He deserves respect for knowing when to retire, and not changing his mind. His 27 wins (two more than Clark) were won in 99 GPs.

2. Niki Lauda

Lauda was just as puny a figure as Stewart and he also had to throw himself on the mercy of others in order to race, although in his case his benefactor was a local bank. The $30,000 credit he raised seemed a hair-raising amount at the time, but others, including Damon Hill, were inspired to follow his example.

Lauda's pushy self-confidence was not arrogance, it was the correct evaluation of his ability. Joining Ferrari in 1974, he allied himself with newly appointed team chief Luca di Montezemolo and used his technical and diplomatic skills to help guide the Scuderia back to success. His famous walkout from Brabham in 1979 was upstaged only by

his return to F1, with McLaren, in 1983. His airline needed the $6 million - and he justified it all when he beat team-mate Alain Prost to the 1984 title at the slowest possible speed.

3. Emerson Fittipaldi

Emerson Fittipaldi ruined a reputation for canniness in one stroke when he opted to drive his own underfunded Copersucar instead of going for what could have been a third World Championship in 1976. Although the project eventually bankrupted him, he would later redeem himself by becoming the respected elder statesman of the CART circuit, with two Indy 500 victories to his credit.

These facts have long since obscured the fact that he was an unusually sensitive driver and the youngest ever world champion (at 25, with Lotus, in 1972). His laid-back 'minimum effort' style and a second title with McLaren in 1974 inspired a flock of Brazilians to follow him into F1. Among his greatest admirers was his country's next World Champion, Nelson Piquet.

4. Jody Scheckter

Jody Scheckter arrived in Europe from South Africa in 1971 with one thousand pounds of scholarship money in his pocket and a reputation for driving

Formula Fords sideways. He retired from racing nine years later with one of the wisest heads in the sport and enough money to start a business which has made him much richer.

Much of Scheckter's savvy was acquired from Denny Hulme, but he also listened to Jackie Stewart. The close friendship he formed with Gilles Villeneuve at Ferrari gave him the World Championship in 1979 without any rancour - and when he walked down the nose of his car as a farewell gesture at Watkins Glen in 1980, the mechanics applauded warmly even though he had taken only two points from the season's 13 races.

5. James Hunt

British motor racing owes a debt to James Hunt for putting the sport on the front page as well as the back. He was helped there by the antics of Lord Hesketh's band of party animals, and by other acts of personal mischief. But the playboy was also an inspired driver

who knew exactly what he wanted to achieve and how hard he would have to work.

Hunt did almost everything right, and not just in terms of satisfying the writers of newspaper headlines. His only serious mistake was to have retired midway through the 1979 season, albeit for reasons which seemed excellent at the time, a career move which left him to the aimlessly wanton existence which contributed to his fatal heart attack in 1993.

6. Jochen Rindt

Orphaned in a wartime raid over Cologne, Jochen Rindt spent his inheritance on racing cars. His money, and his natural talent, may explain the arrogance which some contemporaries saw in him. But he was certainly not

scared. Obsessed about the fragility of his Lotus, he was considering retirement when the car broke for the last time, killing him as he was nudging the limits during a practice session at Monza.

Although his life ended barely eight months into the decade, Rindt was a contemporary (and close friend) of that Seventies man Jackie Stewart. His death at the age of only 28 pushed Stewart to even greater efforts in search of improved safety.

7. Gilles Villeneuve

The four victories which Gilles Villeneuve won for Ferrari in 1978 and 1979 were not perhaps as spectacular as the two which he won in 1981, but they had the same never-say-die quality which would turn the Canadian into a legend.

Honest and fearless, Villeneuve was a straightforward racer who liked nothing better than a wheel-to-wheel battle. His fellow drivers loved him, too, even when he was driving like a hooligan. A light went out when he was killed at Zolder in 1982, trying - as usual - to do the impossible.

8. Ronnie Peterson

For spectacle and commitment, the Seventies had no equal for the sight of Ronnie Peterson pushing mere metal and rubber beyond the limit. Such extraordinary car control entirely forgave his shortcomings in testing and setting up his cars, although there were times when Lotus could have used a more analytical driver.

While the records show 10 victories for Peterson, Sweden's greatest driver will best be remembered for his quick wits and sportsmanship. When he rejoined Lotus in 1978 it was understood, and never challenged, that he would not try to race Mario Andretti. Though he was often faster than the American, Peterson kept his promise without a word of complaint.

9. Mario Andretti

No driver has had a deeper respect for the traditions of the sport than Mario Andretti. As a kid in Italy, desperate to see Ascari driving a Ferrari, he scrambled under a fence at Monza. As a grown man in the USA, with all the money he could ever need coming in from his career driving Indycars, he could not resist the temptation to seek the World Championship.

The title, when it came in 1978, was a well deserved reward for the three years he had spent helping to pull Lotus back into shape. Maybe Andretti lingered too long in Europe

with less worthy teams, but when he finally went home, he did so with the sport's respect for him stronger than ever.

10. Jacky Ickx

Urbane and polite off the track, Jacky Ickx could be frighteningly brave behind the wheel. Equally at home in a sportscar as in an F1, he enjoyed dangerous circuits and was usually unstoppable in the rain. He was consistent and persistent, and rarely ever gave less than his best. Typically, his career continued well into his forties as he took on the challenge of desert raids.

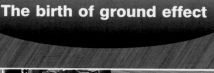

The birth of ground effect

Racing car designers really do dream of stumbling across some brand new engineering principle which will give them an increase in performance that will overwhelm rivals. In the 35 years of his active life, Colin Chapman's fantasies were realised more frequently than anyone else's. When he discovered ground effects, he was happy to call it 'something for nothing.'

Chapman's mind rarely rested, even when he was lying on a beach. In August 1975, while topping up his tan during the annual family holiday in Ibiza, his mind drifted to aerodynamics. Racing cars had carried conventional wings for almost 10 years, but that was not enough for Chapman. He envisaged a racing car which was itself a wing, shaped to generate negative lift from its underside.

Once back home, Chapman called for some studies to be done in a quarter-scale wind tunnel fitted with a moving carpet, to simulate the effect of a car running at speed on the road. One of the engineers involved, Peter Wright, already knew what a fruitful path this would be, having seen the phenomenon while doing some wind tunnel work at BRM and later on a Lotus passenger car.

Wherever the idea really was born, the principles of ground effect that would become familiar in F1 racing had been laid down, with the car's underside profiled to create a venturi 'throat.' Flexible strips (or skirts) would be required to hold in the air, closing the gap between the sides of the car and the road. Perhaps because of journalists' unwillingness to get down on their knees, it was the skirts rather than the shaping of the underside which first attracted the attention of the press.

Lotus' fortunes, both in the showroom and on the race track, had hit new lows in 1975. When the new 1976 car showed itself to be less than a winner, the trusted Tony Rudd got on with the design of a new chassis to incorporate the ideas which he and Wright had developed in the wind tunnel. The result, the Lotus 78, Lotus's first ground effect car, was ready to be tested in August that year. When Gunnar Nilsson drove it in secret at Snetterton, the performance was so electrifying that Chapman decided not to use it until 1977, to prevent his ideas being copied by rival designers during the winter.

The car was certainly good enough to have won the 1977 World Championship for Andretti, who took it to four wins. He also had two silly first lap accidents, but the team's most serious problem was a series of engine failures for which Chapman could never find an explanation. Andretti would have his championship reward in 1978 with the Lotus 79, a svelte-looking refinement of the 78.

Realising that Chapman had made a breakthrough, his more astute rivals were soon at work on copycat designs. Of these, the most significant would be Patrick Head's Williams FW09, the car which made Frank Williams' dreams come true and started his company on the winning road.

With the combined might of F1's design talent exploiting it, ground effects put a premium price on the heads of good aerodynamicists. To the relief of those teams (the majority, even then) which had no alternative to the Cosworth DFV engine, it would provide an instant answer to the threat from the turbo engine introduced by Renault in mid-1977. The British V8, just the right shape to accommodate ground effects, earned a new lease of life which would ensure its success for another six years. So effective was undercar aerodynamics that cornering speeds escalated to the point where the FIA stepped in with the 'flat bottom' regulations that came into effect in 1984. Colin Chapman had died in December 1982 and was not there to protest, as he would surely have done. In a poignant way it was perhaps appropriate that he should have gone to his grave at a moment when his rivals were once again scrambling to catch up with him.

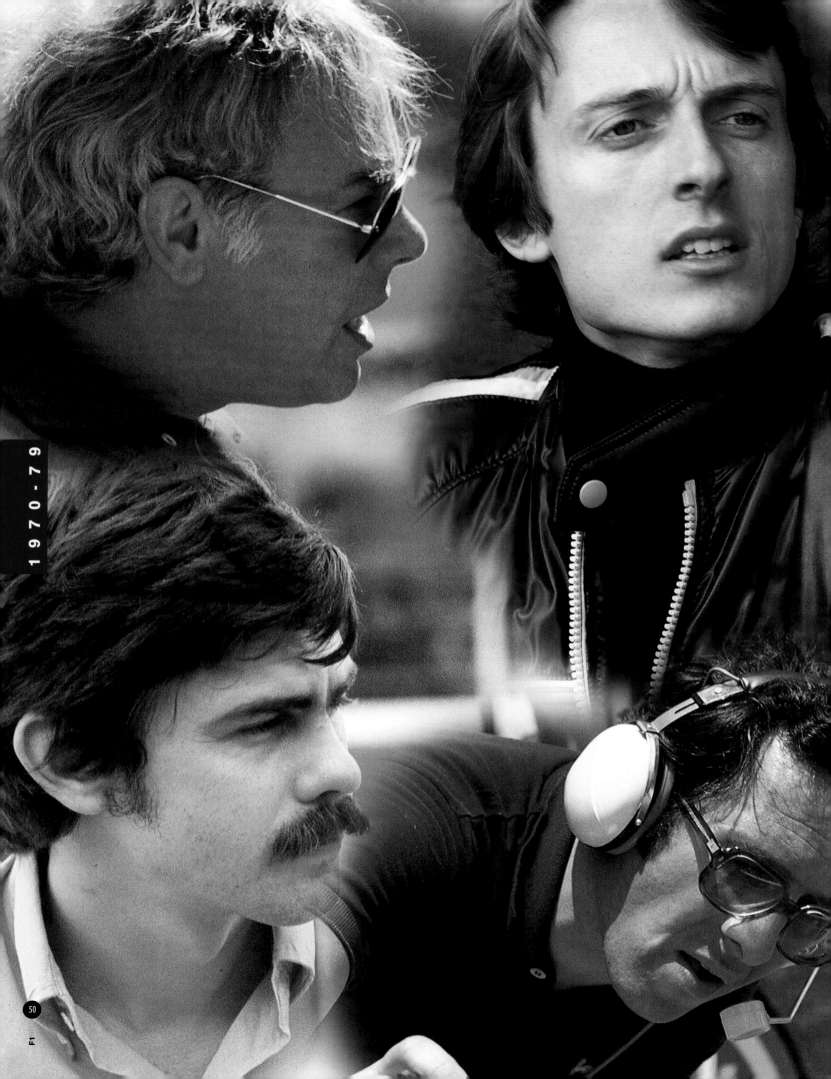

Personalities

Mike Doodson

Mauro Forghieri

With his craggy, lugubrious features and autocratic management style, Mauro Forghieri was the technical heart and soul of Scuderia Ferrari until Harvey Postlethwaite arrived in 1980 with a mission to get things up to date. Mauro's reign included the three seasons when Niki Lauda (1975 and 1977) and Jody Scheckter (1979) secured the team's most recent Drivers' World Championships.

The product of a long-gone era when engineers always overruled drivers, he was the effervescent, arm-swirling all-Italian king of the Ferrari pit who did not hesitate to describe Lauda, to his face, as 'a silly little boy.'

In the aftermath of the famous staff walkout from Maranello in 1961, Forghieri - then still barely three years out of university - was among the young engineers who found themselves instantly promoted to take charge of the design office so suddenly vacated by the equally colourful Carlo Chiti. It was an assignment which in one form or another would last another 18 years.

Mauro's father, a pattern maker with the Scuderia in its pre-war Alfa Romeo days, was still employed in the factory in the early Sixties. Once the boy had earned his Engineering degree, his father sought a position for him, too. As far as Mr Ferrari was concerned, a vital factor was that the youthful Forghieri, like himself, was first and foremost an engine man. And he already had close experience of the Ferrari V6s which imposed themselves on the 1.5-litre F1 introduced in 1961 while the folks at Coventry-Climax and BRM were still sitting on their hands.

By his own admission, Forghieri had to pick up the rudiments of chassis design as he went along, a skill which served him sporadically well throughout the Seventies. As early as the 1968 Belgian GP, he had introduced aerodynamic aerofoils to F1 racing. This was a somewhat ironic bit of pioneering work when you consider that inside Ferrari 10 years later he would be blamed for a rearguard action to resist the attempts of his own design office to copy the aerodynamic innovations of their British rivals in the use of ground effect…

Forghieri's personal masterpiece was the three-litre flat-12 engine which won 37 GPs, and a handful of sportscar races, between 1970 and 1980. Logic says that such a magnificently compact piece of engineering should have won far more

Forghieri's Ferrari flat-12 was the only engine truly capable of challenging the Cosworth FV over the long haul.

races than it did, for it was intrinsically smoother, more reliable and (for most of its life) more powerful than the V8s being churned out by Cosworth for most of the rival teams during the same period. Not many would argue, however, that the 312 B1 chassis which Forghieri also penned for it was the most elegant Grand Prix car of 1970 - or for that matter of any other season since F1 had gone rear-engined.

Although Forghieri's position at Maranello changed constantly, he was never happier than when he was at the track with his cars. Grand Prix cars, F2s, sportscars: he would be in the pits, chastising drivers, mechanics and journalists with the same expressive panache. The sport has since moved on, leaving Forghieri as a freelance consultant whose seat-of-the-pants 'feel' for racing cars no longer, more's the pity, has the same value.

Keith Duckworth

There is no better example of the transformation that has taken place in motor racing during the last quarter century than the story, now virtually a parable, of the three-litre V8 Cosworth DFV (Double Four Valve) engine. Today, a similar project would directly involve a seven-figure sum, at least 50 technicians and weeks on the test bed before the engine was even allowed to start track testing.

In 1966, designer Keith Duckworth spent several lonely months hunched over a drawing board in the spare bedroom of his tiny suburban house in Northampton, toiling late into the night and surviving on a diet of steak and cabbage. It was the first engine he had ever designed from scratch. Although performance exceeded the target of 400 bhp when it was brake tested, it showed signs of an oil breathing problem. With no time to isolate the fault, the Lotus mechanics simply incorporated the pipes and tin boxes lashed around it as a temporary fix.

Not that there is anything slapdash about Duckworth himself, for this is a man who preaches engineering logic with the verve of a born-again evangelist. Before pencil met paper he had spent at least two months contemplating how best to achieve the smallest, lightest 'package.' His idea of using the engine as part of the structure of the car may not have been entirely original (Lancia had done something similar 10 years earlier), but there were many other ingenious details. One of them was his use of the incoming air to cool the fuel in galleries cast into the inlet manifold, a feature which instantly became a fundamental part of racing engine design.

Compared to today, the resources available to Cosworth seem almost pitiful. That first shake-down test was done by Duckworth's partner Mike Costin, a part-time racer. Costin whipped off his jacket, climbed in and had a quick blast around the Hethel airfield circuit owned by Group Lotus. Its first non-stop race distance test was its first Grand Prix, at Zandvoort in Holland on June 4, 1967, in which Jim Clark opened the scoring in an astonishing innings which would eventually stretch to 155 F1 race wins over a period of 17 years.

The cost of the DFV when it became available to selected customer teams in 1968 was a reasonable £7500. Among the entrants who would build their racing empires on this readily available and increasingly powerful unit was Frank Williams. In turbo guise it would become an Indy winner and it was winning Formula 3000 races as recently as 1994. Its progeny - smaller, lighter V8s - only said goodbye to F1 at the end of 1997.

After all four of the original partners had sold their shareholdings in 1980, eventually their old company became part of the Vickers defence group, with interests that extend well beyond just motor racing. When the author visited Cosworth in 1996 it came as a shock that the receptionist had no knowledge of the two engineers whose names had been amalgamated in to create the identity of her employer. Fortunately, Keith Duckworth is to be found at the occasional race, still preaching his principles of good design and commonsense.

Luca di Montezemolo

When you strip away the legends that entwine the great name of Ferrari, what you will find is just another racing team. Bigger, more inscrutable and vastly more complex than any other, it requires a special kind of chief executive. Since the

Clockwise from bottom left: Gordon Murray; Keith Duckworth; Luca di Montezemolo; Mauro Forghieri.

end of 1991, that post has been filled by Luca di Montezemolo. With his dark glasses and tendency towards posturing, this aristocratic-looking bombast isn't universally popular. But the fact remains that nobody has been as good for Ferrari in the last 25 years as he has.

In fact, di Montezemolo had already turned the tables for Ferrari once before. He first arrived at Maranello late in 1973, fresh out of Columbia business school, with the brief - from his mentor, Fiat scion Gianni Agnelli - to rescue the Scuderia from one of its regular muddles. He hired Niki Lauda, marshalled the elements of Mauro Forghieri's scattered genius and supervised the resurgence which delivered Lauda's two titles in 1975 and 1977. When he departed early in 1976 he was still only 26 years old.

Just as he would do with Michael Schumacher 23 years later, Montezemolo forged a close link with Lauda. As he said in 1992, 'I am old in F1 and I cannot forget that the best combination is when a driver and the team can be really one element together.' With his surpassing confidence in his own ability to win races, Lauda needed that sort of support. Montezemolo helped the young Austrian through the minefield of Maranello's politics and allowed him to concentrate on the job of testing and setting up his car, free of outside interference. It helped that Montezemolo, who had no more than a passing interest in racing until he arrived at Ferrari, had no preconceptions about his job. He was lucky enough - or maybe it was his well-developed diplomatic skills that did it – to establish an excellent rapport with Enzo Ferrari. He encouraged Lauda to report directly to Mr Ferrari as soon as possible after each race. Lauda later recalled that he would phone the Old Man early on Mondays after a race, before the newspapers had been delivered to his farmhouse.

When Montezemolo returned in 1991, fresh from organising football's Italia '90 World Cup, it was as President of Ferrari. As one of his own engineers would observe, at first he was not aware of the huge task he had undertaken. Ever since Mr Ferrari had died in 1988 the management had been in the hands of one anonymous Fiat executive after another. Not only was the racing division in disarray following the sacking of Alain Prost at the end of 1990, but the quality of the passenger cars was poor. Sales were in a slump, morale was at rock bottom.

While the quality of the passenger cars is now unequalled, and sales have put the division back into profit, Montezemolo's Mark 2 renaissance is taking longer to achieve on the racing side. There have been two false starts on the engineering side, with both Harvey Postlethwaite and John Barnard deciding to move on. But bringing Michael Schumacher on board in 1996 has given the team back its pride and confidence. Once again, the driver and his team are one element together.

Gordon Murray

Gordon Murray claims that he found employment at Brabham purely by chance as a result of wandering into the factory on an afternoon in 1970 when Ron Tauranac happened to be interviewing candidates for jobs in the drawing office. He would stay for another 18 years, in charge of design throughout the Ecclestone years, until suddenly walking out after a famous row (nothing to do with racing) with the boss in the company car park.

Tall, quiet and still only 26 years old, Murray had come from Durban in South Africa in the hope of persuading Lotus to give him a job designing road cars. Although he had worked as a mechanical draughtsman and studied engineering part-time at Natal Technical College, his most important asset was that he had designed, built and raced his own hillclimb special. He arrived at Brabham at a propitious moment. Ecclestone bought the team in 1971 and Murray became chief designer in 1972.

Ecclestone left him mostly to his own devices, to be rewarded with a series of fast and competitive racing cars. But there was too much cost-cutting (including a spell when the Ford engines were sent to an old bike-tuning mate of Ecclestone's for rebuilding) and Murray was always seriously overworked. It would not be until 1976 that he was given an assistant in the drawing office.

The most spectacular of the Murray Brabhams was the BT46 of 1978, which made the headlines twice: once because it was such an abject failure, then later because it was too successful! Early in 1975 Ecclestone had reached an agreement with Alfa Romeo for a supply of the Italian company's flat-12 engines. Although large, heavy and thirsty, they were also extremely powerful. In 1977 Brabham works driver John Watson was forced out of the French and British GPs with fuel starvation, both times when he had been firmly in command of the races. After two years without a win, for 1978 Murray conceived ground-breaking design, the BT46. It pioneered an integral jacking system and digital instruments, but its most spectacular novelty was a system of surface-mounted cooling panels to replace conventional radiators. When the surface cooling proved inadequate, Murray was undeterred. He revamped the BT46 around an equally controversial cooling system, using a large fan at the rear of the car, driven from the gearbox, to draw air through a radiator mounted horizontally above the engine. Underneath the rear of the car was an arrangement of skirts: when the engine was revved, the effect of the fan was to suck the car visibly close to the road.

A blizzard of protests greeted the car at its first race, in Sweden. All were rejected, and Niki Lauda won comfortably. However, following 'discussions', the BT46 'fan car' never raced again.

Murray did not reap the full rewards for his skills as a racing car designer until the Eighties, when Brabham, Nelson Piquet and, later, BMW got together to take two World Championships. His greatest contribution to automotive history, however, was to be the F1 road car which he designed for McLaren after moving to Woking in 1987. But that's another story.

> 'Ecclestone left him mostly to his own devices, to be rewarded with a series of fast and competitive racing cars'

Lateral thinking epitomised Murray's approach. This is the controversial Brabham fan car.

The Top Five Races

Mike Doodson

Monza 1970

Tragedy on Saturday, triumph on Sunday. Monza always delivers emotion by the bucketful, never more than on this weekend. The old grandstands in their peeling ochre paint face the concrete pits, creating a juxtaposition of noise: the racket of engines at maximum revs flung out as cars dash past, matched by the roar of partisan spectators reacting to the drama unfolding directly in front of them.

That Sunday it was a somewhat muted crowd who filed in. Many wore black ribbons.

The previous afternoon, having been persuaded to do a run with the front and rear wings removed from his Lotus 72, Jochen Rindt had lost control as he braked for the Parabolica. The front of the car was torn off as it struck the guardrail. The driver of the ambulance lost his way to the hospital and Rindt was dead when at last

they arrived. He would become the sport's only posthumous World Champion.

Monza was still without chicanes. The latest rear-engined cars, on wide tyres and with the beginnings of aerodynamic aids, faced the same mixture of flat-out corners which had confronted competitors there in 1926. Now, though, average speeds nudged 150 mph. The Italians had high hopes for Ferrari, whose new 312B with its potent flat-12 engine had found reliability and won its first race three weeks earlier in the hands of Jacky Ickx at the Osterreichring.

A slipstreaming contest was inevitable. Ickx led the first lap and fought hard until eliminated by a broken clutch. Clay Regazzoni, Ferrari's 31 year-old Swiss recruit, now carried all of Italy's hopes. To fight off Jackie Stewart's Tyrrell he had to use some dubious weaving tactics, but the race was handed to him when Beltoise temporarily got his Matra into second

with Fittipaldi, the new World Champion. Between them they would win seven races, but Jackie Stewart scooped the title by winning all five of Tyrrell's victories.

If Fittipaldi was the great strategist, Ronnie was the pole position specialist: he took a record nine of them that year. At Ricard, though, he had to start from the second row due to a mysterious fuel starvation problem. A smart getaway put him in second place behind McLaren's new South African star Jody Scheckter, making his third start in a GP. Scheckter had opted for a low wing set-up which gave him the speed he needed to stay ahead on the Mistral straight, but also made him woefully slow in the corners.

Unable to make an impression on Scheckter, Peterson made the unilateral decision (no radios then) to wave Fittipaldi through. Like every GP at that time, this was a long race without any planned stops for tyres. Ronnie may even have guessed that a duel between the inexperienced South African and a frustrated Brazilian would play in his favour. Fittipaldi saw an opportunity just as they came up to lap Beltoise's BRM. He chanced his arm on the inside line, filling the same piece of road that Scheckter needed to go round Beltoise. The ensuing collision eliminated them both and handed the race to Ronnie, on a plate.

It was a victory which gave as much pleasure to the many fans of the gentle

Rindt's tragedy overshadowed Monza in 1970 (far left); controversy engulfed Brands in 1976 (main picture); and Jody Scheckter led at Ricard in 1973 (above).

place. Regazzoni crammed on all speed to edge away from the Frenchman.

The crowd, deprived of a Ferrari victory at home since 1966, swept on to the track before the race had finished. Late into the night, the cries of 'Re-ga-zzo-nee' would echo off the ancient walls. Jochen Rindt would be remembered, but that night the tifosi had something to celebrate.

Ricard 1973

It was bound to happen sooner or later, and it happened under a fiercely sunny Provencale sky when Ronnie Peterson at last won a Grand Prix - with a little help from the tangle which eliminated Lotus team-mate Emerson Fittipaldi and Jody Scheckter.

Ronnie had joined Lotus from March at the beginning of 1973. So anxious was Colin Chapman to secure the Swede that he promised him equal number one status

Swede as it did to him. He would score another nine GP wins before his death at Monza in 1978, but none of them as easily as this.

Osterreichring 1975

Grand Prix racing was going through a flat patch in 1975. Niki Lauda and Ferrari were lording it over the British opposition, the best of which was provided by Emerson Fittipaldi's McLaren and James Hunt's Hesketh. But you could usually count on Vittorio Brambilla for a bit of light relief, at least until he disappeared, as he so often did, into the scenery.

The March team, managed by an agile-brained ex-barrister called Max Mosley, ran Brambilla's orange car as much on ingenuity as it did on hard cash. When the unpredictable 37 year-old Italian mysteriously took pole position at the Swedish GP it was shamefully alleged that

The writing was already on the wall for forced induction when Fangio's pre-war supercharged Alfetta won the Spanish GP at Pedralbes in 1951. Post-war austerity meant that nobody could afford to build that sort of complex engine anymore and for the next two years F1 races were run for two-litre F2 cars. But there is something so delightfully racy about the word 'supercharged' that the makers of the F1 rules kept it in the regulations right into modern times.

In 1966, when the capacity limit for F1 engines was doubled, to three-litres, provision was made for the old 1.5-litre engines to be supercharged. Still, nobody showed interest. It would be 10 years before Renault, having taken a fresh look at the equivalency rules, concluded that a turbocharged engine could be competitive in F1. A specific F1 project was authorised by the French company in 1976.

Renault, winner of the first ever Grand Prix in 1906, was then in the process of remaking its image in sports car racing, with victory at Le Mans the eventual goal. Its two-litre iron-block V6 engines had started life in normally aspirated guise, contesting the European sportscar championship. Since 1975 they had been equipped with a single Garrett turbocharger and wastegate – and had actually won the first round of that year's championship.

The Renault engineer with the most intimate knowledge of turbocharging was Bernard Dudot, later to head Renault Sport's engine division until 1997. In 1973 Dudot had been sent to California to learn about turbochargers at Garrett AiResearch, before being assigned to the task of sorting out the problems (mostly cracked pistons) which the Le Mans sports cars suffered along the three-mile Mulsanne straight.

Renault had just been defeated again at Le Mans when the Regie's first F1 car was taken to Silverstone for its first F1 race in July 1977. To comply with the equivalency rules, the capacity of the little V6 had been reduced to 1.5-litres, running at 2.8 bar boost (compared with 2.0 bar on the sports car), with a single Garrett turbo spinning at an alarming 130,000 rpm.

The turbo had advantages over the old-fashioned supercharger in terms of weight and complexity, but it suffered a severe handicap in throttle response. In testing at Jarama, driver Jean-Pierre Jabouille complained that on the short straights the braking points came up before the boost came in. The response would be improved by adopting two small KKK turbo units to replace the Garretts.

The turbo engine's early lack of reliability, and the asbestos 'bung' that was stuck up the exhaust pipe to quench the frequent turbo fires, earned Renault more guffaws than laurels. But the team persevered, and by the time Jabouille won the Regie's first GP victory, at Dijon in 1979, rivals were beginning to take turbocharging seriously.

While the expense of forced induction technology had been a deterrent in the past, the arrival of leading car manufacturers had a dramatic effect on budgets in the Seventies. BMW had been involved with F2 racing since 1972 and was also developing turbo engines for touring car events. In 1980, the Munich company announced its intention to develop an F1 engine based on a production iron four-cylinder block.

The French and German companies lavished millions on the struggle to become the first manufacturer to win a turbo World Championship. Intercooling made the engines more driveable, improved materials allowed pistons and rings to withstand huge boost pressures, and complex electronic engine management systems allowed precise fuel metering. In the end, it would be BMW which prevailed. While the Germans concentrated on supplying engines to Bernie Ecclestone's compact Brabham team, Renault's factory operation was smothered by corporate politics. The showdown would be the South African GP of 1983, where Alain Prost's Renault expired with the failure of a cheap but tiny part while the BMW-engined Brabhams dominated the race.

It would be 1986 before Renault learned its lesson from that debacle and opted to concentrate on making and supplying engines to customer teams. The company can take the credit, though, for its pioneering work on turbos, and for changing the face of F1 forever.

someone might have helped improve his time by flashing a clipboard over the timing light.

The drivers, already unnerved by an accident on race morning which would cost the life of the American Mark Donohue, were apprehensive when torrential rain fell shortly before the start. They went to the line on full wets and the race started normally. Soon, though, the rain intensified. When Hunt was inadvertently blocked by his own team-mate, Brambilla gratefully snatched the lead. The race still had 35 laps to go. His mechanics gnawed their fingernails, sure he would make a mistake. But when the weather took another turn for the worse, out came the chequered flag. Brambilla came round, having led the race for 11 laps.

Coming up to the line he was waving madly with one arm. As he crossed it, his car had started to wobble. Only yards later, still doing 140 mph, it snapped sideways, then pirouetted into the mist and spray. The clang as it hit the guardrail could be heard and felt all the way down pit lane. Given that the race had not lasted 60 per cent of the distance, it would only be a half points win. But when Brambilla, unhurt and grinning, returned to the pits in his grubby orange overalls, nothing mattered. It had been the upset of the season.

Brands Hatch 1976

It was when the beer cans started raining over the fence that we knew James Hunt had become a star. A first corner shunt had forced the race to be stopped, officials were dithering over the rules about spare cars and the word was spreading through the public enclosures that James - suddenly he was 'Our' James - might not be allowed to take the restart in his McLaren.

The battle for the 1976 World Championship had not yet reached its peak when Lauda and Hunt arrived at Brands Hatch for the British GP. The Austrian had won four GPs to Hunt's two and nobody would know that only two weeks later Lauda would be horribly injured at the Nurburgring. The British had turned out in record numbers to hail Hunt, whose off-track activities were bringing him more attention in the dailies than his driving.

With the crowd ready to riot and preparing to follow the cans over the barriers, it was hastily decided to let Hunt start regardless. At the restart, 'Our' James lagged a little and he didn't start to attack Lauda until the halfway point. It was the tyres, he explained: he had started with a stagger problem which wore off as the race progressed.

That last half of the race was spellbinding. Trading fastest laps, Hunt closed on his Austrian rival. With 21 laps to go, he attacked the Ferrari on the inside at the Druid's hairpin and slipped through. He would be the first Englishman to have won the British GP since Peter Collins in 1958.

More than two months later, over a green baize table in Paris, it was decided that Hunt should not, after all, have been allowed to start the race. By then, though, he had won another two races and he was making his bid for the 1976 title. Whatever officialdom might decree, Brands had been his finest day.

James Hunt and Tom Pryce flank a delirious Vittorio Brambilla after his surprise win in Austria in 1975 (far left, top and middle). At Dijon four years later Jean-Pierre Jabouille's first win was overshadowed (left and above) by the second place fight between Rene Arnoux and Gilles Villeneuve.

Dijon 1979

The record books show that the first World Championship F1 race to have been won by a turbocharged car was the French Grand Prix at Dijon in 1979. Driving a copybook race for Renault, Jean-Pierre Jabouille was beaten away from the start by the Ferrari 312 T4 of Gilles Villeneuve. The Frenchman held station for 46 laps, then snapped past on the straight prior to securing a serene 15s win.

No debut success could have happened at a more appropriate venue than here at home for Renault. The champagne was waiting, the company executives had their speeches prepared. Above all, Jabouille was entitled to feel that he deserved such a

reward for his loyalty to Renault through two years of disappointment with the fickle turbo.

Instead, all the attention and plaudits would fall on the men who had fought for second place. Their battle had occupied only five laps, but it had been the clash of the decade, if not of the century. Wheel-to-wheel confrontations are to be expected in bike racing or Formula Ford, but not in F1. Yet Gilles Villeneuve and Rene Arnoux had passed and repassed so frequently in those hectic laps that nobody could say how many times they had changed places.

Only special circumstances could have led to such a battle. And it has to be said

that Villeneuve and Arnoux had been in trouble with their cars. For the Canadian it was worn Goodyears, wilting under the stress of holding off Jabouille. For Arnoux, it was his engine. Though his Michelins remained fresh to the end, there was a problem with the fuel system which momentarily killed the Renault V6.

In the end, it was Villeneuve who fended off the Frenchman's hiccoughing turbo and deprived Renault of a possible 1-2 result. Jabouille was on the top step of the podium, but the cheers were for the next two men to finish. Unjust? Maybe. But for a rare moment of motor racing history, it was the sport which had triumphed.

The phantom pragmatist

Helmut Zwickl

Niki Lauda is undoubtedly today's best-known living Austrian. The high points and disasters of his life have attracted worldwide interest. As a child he was shy and something of a weakling, with a fear of horses. Had his opponents ever known that they could have put him out of action with a cat, because of his allergy to them, F1 paddocks would have been crammed with feline forms.

Thanks to his analytical mind and supernatural willpower, able to assess each risk intuitively and with complete emotional detachment, this young man who hadn't had an especially good education, went on to become a three-time World Champion. But it was off the race track that he was to show what he was really capable of. With Lauda-Air he established a respected airline, after a bitter struggle against the monopoly of Austrian Airlines. It was a conflict with the power of the state which, predictably, he finally won. And because he knew that he would only be able to win this fight as a world celebrity and not as a retired racing driver, he took the wholly pragmatic decision to start his racing career for a second time.

Lauda did not begin by racing go-karts, the traditional starting point for so many of today's F1 drivers. Instead he bought a Mini-Cooper for his first race. When he

graduated to Formula 3 and failed, he told himself: 'The risk is too high, because you get nothing but lunatics on the grid. Formula Three isn't getting me anywhere.'

At first, he didn't have sponsors, so he had to finance his entry into Formula 2, one step below F1, with loans. In the 1971 European Formula 2 Championship he only managed to gain 10th place with his works-entered March. It cost him £8000, his car had a lot of ridiculous mechanical faults and he experienced the same as would later happen to Nigel Mansell: The money ran out before he was able to prove to the world that he was a potential champion.

Lauda's self-confidence was quite

After his brilliant recovery in 1976, Lauda was not afraid to withdraw from the rain in Fuji.

remarkable. Only one person really believed in him - Niki Lauda himself. And while driving alongside the highly rated Swedish driver Ronnie Peterson in the March Formula 2 team, he came to the conclusion: 'I must go into Formula 1!' That stubborn self-belief paid off. Nobody could talk him out of his plans. For the Austrian Grand Prix in 1971 he bought a Formula 1 March drive for £2,000. Not only did his Cosworth engine break down in practice, but he also had to hand over his replacement engine to Peterson, whose engine had also suffered mechanical failure. Lauda was thus given the oldest engine, which was rusting in the transporter - the one he'd last raced in a starting line up alongside Jackie Oliver. Lauda recalls:

'March was only interested that I managed to make it five metres from the start, because that meant an immediate bonus from the major sponsor, STP....' After 20 laps he had to give up because of engine failure. In 1972, with further loans, he managed to buy himself fulltime into the March Formula 1 team. By the end of a largely unimpressive season he had no contract and debts amounting to around £100,000. Nevertheless, in 1973 he bought himself into the BRM team, with money that wasn't his. Subsequently he admitted: 'It was all a bluff.'

This time Lauda was able at last to show his true form, and put in a series of strong performances in a relatively uncompetitive car. Enzo Ferrari was impressed as he watched him on television in the Monaco Grand Prix, and told his people: 'We must have this guy!' So for 1974, when Luca di Montezemolo was given the task of sharpening up the team, Lauda became the key figure at Ferrari. He wasn't yet ready to take the title - but he won his first Grand Prix in Spain and repeated the success in Holland. Meanwhile he learned, observed, gave technical guidance, coordinated, motivated and prepared.

'March was only interested that I managed to make it five metres from the start...'

At the beginning of the 1975 season the general opinion was that Niki Lauda would not be able to take that year's championship, either. As the Grand Prix circus made its way from Argentina to Brazil and South Africa and back to Europe, he had won just five World Championship points. But then with typical aplomb Lauda took control of the situation. When Ferrari needed titanium parts, for example, he would phone up BMW in Munich to get hold of them from Germany.

The Seventies were turbulent years for Formula 1. They were marked by bad accidents, strikes, regulatory chaos and too little effort to ensure driver safety. 'We had to live with the fact that every year two people had to die,' Niki recalls. In Barcelona there was a drivers' strike because the safety guard rail hadn't been secured properly. Emerson Fittipaldi gave the organisers an ultimatum: 'As long as the safety rails remain unsecured, we are not going to practice.' Lauda, ever the pragmatist, took the argument to its logical

➡️

No stopping Niki: Zolder '75.

Michelin beats radial prejudice

Just as there had been resistance to slick (grooveless) tyres in 1971 (some leading F1 drivers imagined they would be 'too slippery'), so also were there doubts about the relevance of radials to motor racing. Anybody who had driven a passenger car on the popular Michelin 'X' tyre knew that although the grip was superior, the breakaway was more sudden than on the good old predictable bias-ply tyre. Under the stress of racing, it was widely believed, the loss of grip would be even more violent.

When Michelin arrived on the Grand Prix scene with Renault in 1977, such concerns evaporated. The Renaults with their unreliable turbo engines regularly expired in clouds of steam and smoke, but the drivers seemed delighted with the tyres. Developed from the equipment used by Renault in sportscar racing since 1974, they were sufficiently impressive to persuade Ferrari to switch from Goodyear to Michelin for 1978.

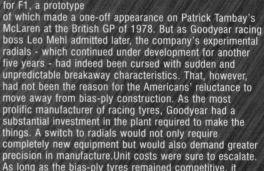

As it happened, Goodyear was already secretly developing radials for F1, a prototype of which made a one-off appearance on Patrick Tambay's McLaren at the British GP of 1978. But as Goodyear racing boss Leo Mehl admitted later, the company's experimental radials - which continued under development for another five years - had indeed been cursed with sudden and unpredictable breakaway characteristics. That, however, had not been the reason for the Americans' reluctance to move away from bias-ply construction. As the most prolific manufacturer of racing tyres, Goodyear had a substantial investment in the plant required to make the things. A switch to radials would not only require completely new equipment but would also demand greater precision in manufacture.Unit costs were sure to escalate. As long as the bias-ply tyres remained competitive, it made sense to stay with the old technology.

Bias-ply also offered benefits that radials did not. The bias-ply would 'grow' while being scrubbed in, and minor variations in the manufacturing process led to some tyres being larger than others. With his experience of high-speed ovals as an Indy car driver, Mario Andretti knew just how to exploit this 'stagger,' which contributed to his World Championship success in 1978.

Meanwhile, Goodyear persevered with its research on radials. 'I guess what finally did the trick was when it rained during an untimed practice session at the 1983 Detroit Grand Prix,' Mehl recalled. 'Not only was Michelin much faster than we were, but so was Pirelli - on cars which were normally slower. As I recall, we were about seven seconds off the pace, so there remained no further doubts that we had to go radial.'

Ferrari had returned to the Goodyear fold in 1982, prompting the company to capitalise on its investment in the historic marque and its founder. A splendid television commercial was made for the US market, featuring idealised tortuous but traffic-free Italian roads, with the Old Man's smiling face superimposed in shot. 'Every Ferrari leaves the factory on Goodyear tyres,' purred the message: 'Mr Ferrari wouldn't want it any other way ...'

Mr Ferrari's choice of tyre has been amply justified by the fickleness of the rival brands. Michelin withdrew at the end of 1984 but may finally return next year. Pirelli, with only one two victories to celebrate since its first return in 1981, retired at the end of 1986. After returning in 1989 the Italian company was gone again at the end of 1991, with only a handful of valiant second places to celebrate.

This season an item of F1 tyre technology turns full circle with the new regulations banning the racing slick and requiring tread patterns. Goodyear and Bridgestone, F1's two suppliers since 1997, confusingly disagree on the value of the new rules to the development of their products. Indeed, Goodyear is finally set to withdraw at the end of the year. Neither company would deny, however, that racing has been good for their image.

conclusion. 'The point is not to discuss what should have been done,' he said, 'but whether we are going to drive or not.' Ken Tyrrell and Bernie Ecclestone, who owned the Brabham team at that time, wanted to send their mechanics out on the track to fix the safety barrier. Lauda could see that a battle of wills was about to take place and he predicted: 'This time the bosses will lose.'

He was wrong. The organisers threatened to have all racing cars and transporters confiscated or impounded within the old Olympic Stadium in which the paddock was located. The team bosses made the consequences clear to the drivers and strike unity dissolved. Lauda was told by his team boss Montezemolo: 'If you don't drive, you're fired.' Gritting his teeth, he resumed practice. Only Fittipaldi had the courage to stay away from the race, in which Rolf Stommelens's Hill flew over the safety barrier and killed five people. The

drivers were helpless puppets and Niki needed first and foremost to work his way up to world stardom before he could express his real views.

That season he was suspended between heaven and hell, a state which only the Ferrari team is capable of producing. He felt the full force of the Italian press, which was largely responsible for the mood of the team, and he had to learn to shield himself from it, by constructing his famously cool exterior. He won the Grands Prix of Monaco, Belgium, Sweden, France and the US and became World Champion with Ferrari.

After five victories in the 1976 season disaster struck. Three days before the accident at the Nurburgring, he had a terrible premonition. On August 1st, while he was driving me round the track in a Fiat, he stopped 6.5 miles out - incredibly enough where the accident was to happen - to point out the Nürburgring's dangers.

faced with the rain-soaked chaos of the Japanese Grand Prix, he threw in the towel. His eyelids were not properly healed, and he told people he had taken the courageous decision: 'Because my life is more important to me than the championship.' So he enabled James Hunt to become World Champion by a one point margin. And he was torn apart by the media as was Michael Schumacher was after the 1997 Grand Prix of Europe, when he lost the fight for the championship against Villeneuve. To those who couldn't understand, including members of the Ferrari team, Lauda was a coward.

In 1977, after he won the World Championship for the second time, he was suddenly the greatest again. In 1978, when he changed to Brabham, Enzo Ferrari branded him a traitor, because he was the first driver who had given him notice to quit. Then suddenly, on September 28th 1979, partway through practice for the Canadian GP in Montreal, he announced that he was quitting. 'I don't want to drive in circles any more,' he said. 'I have no motivation left.'

Lauda had found a new interest, and all his efforts were needed to build up Lauda Air, in which he invested all his personal wealth. Immediately he embarked upon the struggle against the state-owned airline monopoly, but gradually he came to appreciate that it could only be won from a position of strength. So in 1982 he decided to succumb to Ron Dennis' frequent blandishments and make a comeback with McLaren. But there was something else which had contributed to his decision to re-enter the fray, something which allowed Dennis to talk him round: John Barnard built him the first full monocoque made of carbon fibre:

There were embankments, ditches all over the place, no run-off areas. It was a medieval race track, which nowadays wouldn't be acceptable. During the race, Niki hit the same bank which we had stopped by. Possibly because the Ferrari's suspension broke. His fuel tanks exploded in the impact and he was trapped, sitting in the middle of a fireball. The monocoque chassis were made of aluminium at that time, as thin as tin foil in comparison with today's carbon fibre protection which had yet to be harnessed for motor racing. Rescued by the heroic efforts of fellow drivers Arturo Merzario, Brett Lunger, Harald Ertl and Guy Edwards, he struggled for survival for four days in intensive care.

Already written off by Ferrari, who had replaced him with Carlos Reutemann, Lauda fought back to partial fitness in time for the Italian GP at Monza early in September. With a burnt face, scarred for the rest of his life, he became the new phantom of the race track. 'I was terribly scared,' he confessed. But he overcame his fear and took fourth position. Later that season he remained in contention for the championship until,

'For me this was like life insurance,' Niki confirmed. But in the latter half of his 'second career', he would discover that team-mate Alain Prost had the better of him. During practice he could rarely match Prost's speed, 'So knowing that I could not beat him there, I concentrated on the race.' It was a tactic that Prost himself would sometimes employ when he and Ayrton Senna were team-mates at McLaren later that decade.

In 1984 Lauda became World Champion for the third time, beating Prost by half a point, the smallest margin of victory in the championship's illustrious history. Then, at the end of 1985, he took off his helmet for good.

In many respects Niki Lauda was a pioneer. He was the first to have his own therapist and fitness specialist in Willy Dungl, who is reckoned to be Austria's number one health guru. Niki was not an athlete, but he trained hard.

1984, and the narrowest title win of all time.

As a pilot he is outstanding. A Boeing director once said that Lauda was one of the best pilots who had ever been through his company's training. The crash of one of the Lauda-Air Boeings over Thailand was one of the biggest setbacks of his life. Yet only a week after that misfortune he started to overcome it and this charismatic

Ten years earlier (above and left), Ferrari number 12 had thrilled the fans as Lauda's hunger for a first victory pushed him to the limits.

After driving 40 laps he would be in much better condition than his opponents, who, at that point in a race, started to slow as they tired. As far as possible, Niki reduced risk with his capacity for analytical thought - he managed to solve a lot of problems literally before they arose. He also worked on his car until he thought everything was about as good as it could be. His intelligence and his brilliance on the track made him a winner just as he is now in the air.

man showed that he was able to move mountains. Nobody else would have been able to put so much pressure on Boeing to force them to find out what had caused the accident. And because it transpired that the accident had been caused by in-flight failure of the reverse thrust control, new safety systems were put in place to obviate the chance of such terrible disasters in the future.

After Lauda came the computer and kart generation. They said that, in any case, Niki didn't need computers, he was so like one himself. But today when critics suggest that F1 is a nursery school devoid of characters, he has a simple reply. 'You have to give them time. It takes a long time for character to form.' Maybe so, but the sport is unlikely ever to see another Niki Lauda.

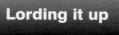

If anyone dared to claim today that it was possible to go Grand Prix racing for fun, how long would it be before the men in white coats arrived? Even in 1973, when Hesketh Racing made its merry GP debut at Monaco, there were those who disapproved. Three years later the noble Lord Hesketh was on his knees financially. But when the party finally ended, His Lordship had earned the gratitude of the nation by delivering a future world champion.

James Hunt's career as an F3 driver was heading rapidly downwards on the day in 1971 when Bubbles Horsley sought him out. Both men were taking part in an F3 race at Chimay in Belgium, and the encounter took place in the tent that passed for the gents' toilet in the middle of a muddy field. Hunt rapidly agreed to drive one of the horrid Dastle F3 cars which Horsley was running for his friend Hesketh.

Obviously Hesketh knew what he was doing when he hired Hunt, although the logic of the match remains far from clear. Fuelled by their common tastes for champagne and fast women, Hunt's star quality flourished and Hesketh's inheritance took a hammering. Two years later, having failed to make any real impression on F2 racing, they took the logical next step and Hesketh bought a Grand Prix car from March.

Arriving at Monaco for their first race, Hesketh and his entourage inspired mixed feelings. TV presenter Barrie Gill, wearing his journalist's hat, claimed - allegedly - to be scandalised to see Hesketh playing fast and loose with tradition. A week later, now sporting his PR agency's headwear, Gill was busy promoting the interests of his new client, one Lord Hesketh.

Memories burn bright of the pranks and excesses in which Hesketh's band of Hooray Henrys indulged. They invited rock stars and celebrity chefs to the races (just as today's far more staid F1 teams do). Bubbles, well ahead of his time, drummed up financial support from supporters by offering a range of knicks-knacks and clothing emblazoned with a jolly Hesketh teddy bear. There was an embarrassing legal moment when it turned out that the bear symbol belonged to somebody else.

Hesketh ensured that the quality of the racing management was copper bottomed. While Horsley imposed a strict discipline on his team, Dr Harvey Postlethwaite - who had come from March - proved to be an ambitious and ingenious chief engineer. In 1974 Hesketh's money enabled him to design his very first GP car, the Hesketh 308. It was a winner, too.

First time out in competition, in the Race of Champions at Brands Hatch, James put it on the pole. There was greater glory to come in another non-championship event, the International Trophy at Silverstone. Again Hunt was on pole, 1.7s faster than Ronnie Peterson's Lotus. But it all went wrong at the start, with the clutch slipping and the protective knob being wrenched off the gear lever.

James was 15th at the end of the first lap. With the clutch pedal useless, he attacked hard. By lap five he was fifth, by lap 13 he was second behind Peterson. Would he dare to challenge the Swede, the fastest driver in the world? You bet. Completing 28 laps, James made his move at the place where Peterson least expected it. Woodcote corner in 1974 was just as it had been when the old Silverstone airfield was opened for racing in 1948, a glorious flat-out right-hander, unsullied by chicanes or kerbs. James, attacking on the inside, somehow made it through by using the grass on the inside. Nobody could remember anyone pulling off anything like that at that corner.

By 1975, the team's third in F1, Hunt would collect points in eight world championship races. His debut victory, at Zandvoort, was to be the only Grand Prix win for Hesketh, but it was no walkover. Niki Lauda, on his way to his second title with Ferrari, admitted that he had been outdriven by the Englishman in the tricky wet/dry conditions.

Two months later, on a cold October afternoon at Thruxton, Hesketh and Hunt said goodbye to their loyal British public. The money had run out and the team was for sale.

A decade of growth

Joe Saward

Grand Prix racing has always been a world where change is constant. F1 people always say that unless you are running forwards you are dropping behind because everyone in the sport is sprinting just to stand still. There is a tendency to think that all change is for the worst but this is not always the case. The Eighties saw F1 boom and yet, at the same time, the number of fatal accidents dived. The sport became infinitely safer than it had been. One can only say that this was progress.

Perhaps improved safety came at the price of changes to the circuits and less spectacular cars, but keeping up with the technical progress being made by the engineers became more and more difficult as better and brighter minds came into the sport, attracted by its excitement and by the potential earnings a good engineer could generate. At the start of the Eighties there were a few million dollar drivers; by the end of the decade there were several million dollar engineers. By then the drivers were earning vast sums, into the tens of millions.

The money came from the growth of the sport. Big sponsors arrived and with them came the motor manufacturers. More money funded a better and more professional show, but it also brought greater pressure for success and so the ethics of the game slipped a little. Drivers showed that they were willing to drive one another off the track to win World Championships. There was precious little room left for gentlemanly behaviour.

Off the track gentlemanly behaviour was equally hard to find. Money became the driving force in the F1 paddock and the decade began with an unseemly and damaging battle between the Federation Internationale du Sport Automobile (FISA) and the Formula 1 Constructors' Association (FOCA) over who should have commercial control of Grand Prix racing. This became universally known as The FISA/FOCA War.

The FISA controlled the promotional rights but FOCA wanted to grab them. The political battles lasted until March 1981 when both sides realised that they would

Turbos rule: Piquet, Brabham and BMW were always quick (left), while Alboreto and Lauda fought hard in 1984 (bottom) and Mansell (above) won his first race at Brands in 1985.

have to compromise. FOCA had tried to put together a breakaway series and had failed, FISA had tried to run races without the FOCA teams but these had been embarrassing. And so a compromise was agreed and the Concorde Agreement came into being.

This contract - signed by all the teams and the governing body - guaranteed that FISA would keep control of the rights but

'Years later it was revealed that the fuel used that autumn was, quite literally, rocket fuel'

would allow FOCA to exploit them in exchange for a considerable annual income. Everyone was happy.

The Concorde Agreement was to provide the foundation for the growth of the sport for the next 15 years. The exploitation of the promotional rights was left largely to Bernie Ecclestone as the other teams were too busy trying to win races to care. They did not want to take such commercial risks and, as a result, gradually over the next few years FOCA agreed to subcontract a lot of the work to Ecclestone's private company Formula 1 Promotions and Administration. The teams were happy as their share of the money was always on the increase. The FISA was making money, and Ecclestone was making plenty and gradually taking over all commercial aspects of the sport.

The growth in TV viewing was dramatic. In 1981 an estimated 8.5 billion people watched F1 racing. By 1990 this figure had risen to 17.6 billion. The really dramatic growth would not come until the early Nineties when the figures rocketed to 45 billion.

The political stability after the Concorde Agreement coincided with the turbocharged era in Grand Prix racing when horsepower figures rose to phenomenal levels, the BMW qualifying engines in the mid-Eighties reckoned to be producing close to 1500 bhp, almost one horsepower for each cubic

centimetre. The chassis regulations limited the amount of downforce available and so the cars were wonderfully overpowered and spectacular to watch as drivers struggled to master them. The race to develop more power was an exciting one not just for the engine manufacturers but also for the oil companies, which took drastic steps forward with the composition of F1 fuels. BMW worked closely with BASF offshoot Wintershall and produced a remarkable fuel which, quite literally, blew away the opposition at the end of 1983. The FISA said it was legal. Years later it was revealed that the fuel used that autumn was, quite literally, rocket fuel and had been developed at the German rocket research centre at Peenemunde during World War II. The formula had been locked away for nearly 40 years...

But even with rocket fuels such progress would not have been possible without electronic management systems, an area where Grand Prix racing made leaps and bounds forward in the Eighties. Although it is generally accepted these days that racing does not greatly improve the average road car, there is little doubt that some of the electronic research has been very important for the motor industry in the Nineties.

It was not just the motor manufacturers who poured money into the sport ; major sponsors paid ever larger amounts for the exposure which F1 boasted around the world. This was particularly useful for the cigarette companies. In the late Seventies only Marlboro and Gitanes were involved in any large way in the sport but in the Eighties they were joined by JPS and Rothmans (1982), Barclay and Skoal Bandit (1984), West (1985) and Camel (1987). They did not all stay in the business, although by the beginning of the Nineties F1's dependence on cigarette money was becoming more and more obvious.

The vast sums of money coming in to F1 enabled the established teams to invest in impressive industrial infrastructure. The era of the small team putting together a kit-car with a 475 bhp Ford DFV engine in the back was over. The top teams of the late

http://www.F150.com

F150

Senna dominated Monaco in 1988, until his embarrassing late-race gaffe.

Eighties were all equipped with their own carbon composite facilities, autoclaves, wind tunnels and advanced computerised machinery.

Not all the teams could cope with such growth. Some rode the wave of progress with ease - Williams and McLaren in particular emerging as the potent new forces, but other big names such as March, Brabham and Lotus failed to capitalise on the situation and began to fade away.

Brabham's slow decline can, in part at least, be traced to Ecclestone's increased involvement in the promotion of the sport, which left him less time to run his team. When sponsorship and a new engine could not be found for the team in 1988 he simply pulled it out of F1. It came back later under different ownership but it would never recover the same status and it went sadly into ruined in the early Nineties before dying altogether.

Ferrari re-invented itself several times in the course of the Eighties. After producing wonderful engines but dreadful chassis in the early part of the decade, Enzo Ferrari was convinced to hire Englishmen to build chassis for him. Harvey Postlethwaite's 126C2 and C3 designs won the team the Constructors' titles in 1982 and 1983 but after that no team other than Williams and McLaren won a Constructors' title until Benetton in 1995 - a run of 11 years during which McLaren won six and Williams five titles.

Ferrari turned to another Englishman, John Barnard, and gave him free rein, even allowing him to establish a Ferrari facility in England, but the death of Enzo in 1988 undermined Barnard and the project eventually foundered. After Ferrari's death Ferrari reinvented itself in Fiat form but after several failures turned to an old Ferrari hand from the Seventies, Luca di Montezemolo, who took over as president

of Ferrari at the end of 1991.

By the end of the Eighties Britain was completely dominant as the centre of the motor racing industry. The highly specialised skills in composite technology could not be found on The Continent and the network between the British teams meant that whenever there was a major development they were all ahead of the European teams. It was no coincidence that the small European teams either died out or had their cars built in Britain. And around the Grand Prix teams developed a network of specialist suppliers and the motor racing industry grew to such an extent that it became in the late Eighties one of the few British success stories at a time when many industries were cutting back. The need to be competitive gave it a constant edge.

Despite the growth Formula 1 stood for technical excellence right through the Eighties and refused to be drawn down the path to a more show business approach to racing. This would happen in the Nineties

BMW's cam covers said it all.

with the introduction of pace cars and pit stops. There were briefly pit stops in 1982 and 1983 but the clever tactic, pioneered by Brabham, was outlawed at the end of 1983 because of the inherent dangers.

Safety was certainly an area in which Grand Prix racing progressed well in the Eighties. In part this was due to the introduction of carbon composite technology, which made the cars a great deal stronger, but some of the praise must also go to Jean-Marie Balestre, the mercurial president of the FISA, who refused to listen to the teams and took action when he felt things were getting out of control.

The ground-effect era, which lasted between 1978 and 1982, saw the cars able to corner ever more quickly, and as a result suspensions became harder and harder. In the end drivers were suffering injury just from driving the cars over bumps. At the end of 1982, as the turbocharged engines began to make more of an impact, Balestre pushed through regulations introducing flat bottomed cars and banning skirts. In addition the size of the rear wings was reduced. It meant a reduction of around 60 percent of the downforce at the time - but it was not long before the engineers began to win that back. In addition Balestre insisted on increased frontal protection for drivers.

When turbocharging reached those extraordinary levels of horsepower, Balestre acted again - not only to drop speeds but also to reduce the investment needed for F1. The turbos were gradually strangled by fuel limitations and by the 1989 season turbocharging had been banned and everyone switched over to 3.5 litre normally aspirated engines. Balestre had wanted V8s only but Enzo Ferrari insisted on V12s. As a result the door was left open for V10 engines, which quickly became the best compromise.

Balestre continued to push through new

testing the sport lost Elio de Angelis in May 1986, though the Brabham driver would probably have lived but for scandalously poor marshalling which meant he was not released from his upturned car and died of asphyxiation when a small fire deprived him of air. It was a lesson that should have been learned after the Williamson accident at Zandvoort in 1973. Scandalous, too, were the circumstances under which the French driver, Philippe Streiff, became paralysed after a testing accident in Rio early in 1989, from which he had initially walked away.

Although the teams often grumbled at Balestre's reforms, he generally got what he wanted. By the end of the Eighties, however, the bigger of them had been riding a pleasant circle upwards. Success attracted money. This was invested in more research and development and thus these teams became even more successful. The rest were left to struggle in the vicious circle. After the crash of 1989 a lot of the smaller F1 teams disappeared but a core of well-funded and relatively well-run operations remained as the decade came to a close.

Perhaps at the end of the decade life in the F1 paddock was less fun than it had been. There was much more that needed to be done. There were many more journalists than ever before; there were more sponsors; drivers had to spend hours with their engineers analysing data and so contact with the media and with the public became increasingly difficult. But one thing remained the same: in the time between the green lights (they still had them in the Eighties) and the chequered flag the drivers still gave everything - no matter what the machinery they were driving nor the amount of money they were earning. And in such a constantly changing world, it was good to know that the competitive spirit of the sport lived on.

safety items until the end of the decade and in 1989 insisted upon larger cockpit openings, better rearward visibility, higher rollhoops, reinforced lateral protection for drivers and mandatory and intensive chassis crash testing.

The FISA president was always very proud of his safety record and there is no doubt that some of his rule changes - although unpopular with the teams - did improve the situation. After Gilles Villeneuve and Riccardo Paletti died in 1982, there was not a single fatality at an F1 race meeting until Imola in 1994. But in

'After the crash of 1989 a lot of the smaller F1 teams disappeared'

Team orders have never been a strong feature of Williams' team management strategy.

Carbon-fibre technology

As long ago as the late Thirties composite materials began to be used in aviation. Multi-millionaire Howard Hughes used a plastic-impregnated wood material for his famous flying boat Spruce Goose, but material development did not really accelerate until the late Fifties when the space programme in the United States began to look for light, strong and stable materials. The composites produced were enormously expensive but gradually began to sneak into Formula 1 in the mid-Seventies. The wing strut which Broke on Rolf Stommelen's Hill GH1 at Montjuich Park in the 1975 Spanish Grand Prix was made of carbon fibre.

Such materials began to replace the classic aluminium sheet monocoques which F1 designers had been building for almost 15 years. Gradually sheet aluminium was replaced by aluminium sheet covering metal honeycomb and then by composite-covered honeycomb panels which were bonded together. By 1979 Gordon Murray's Brabham BT49 was largely made out of such carbon composite materials. It was the McLaren MP4/1, designed by John Barnard which was the first all-composite chassis. Lotus was not far behind with its twin-chassised 88, although this was later banned by the FISA.

The McLaren MP4/1 weighed in at about 44 lb, which was 40 percent lighter than the aluminium sandwich cars, but a great deal more expensive. Not only were the materials expensive but the chassis had to be built in America by aerospace company Hercules. But it was competitive, as John Watson proved by winning the British Grand Prix in July that year. It was also strong: Andrea de Cesaris, Watson's team-mate, crashed an embarrassing number of times that year without doing himself any harm.

The success led others to follow suit and in 1982 Gerard Ducarouge's Alfa Romeo and Rory Byrne's Toleman were both composite chassis. In 1983 ATS designer Gustav Brunner made another smallbreakthrough when he designed the first composite chassis which did not have external bodywork. This took the chassis weight down to just 39 lb. That same year Brabham, Ferrari, Renault and others switched to composite chassis, though it would be 1985 before Williams had enough faith in the new materials to build its first.

The new chassis designs created whole new areas of research for F1 engineering teams and stress analysis became an important new field.

Working with composites is now done in-house by almost all the racing teams and they lead the world in such technology. It remains something of a cottage industry with laminators still laying out carbon 'cloth' impregnated with resin in female moulds of the planned chassis. The cloths have to be laid in the correct orientation and at the correct thickness so that all the loadings, calculated by the designers, will be in the right directions. The chassis is then heated in a vacuum autoclave. The production processes develop each year but the basic skills remain. Computers and machines can replace most things in F1, but it will be a long time before the laminators find themselves looking for work...

Immovable object

Prost (left) and Senna (right), were simply too alike in many ways for their own good.

Gerald Donaldson

To understand the reasons for the feud between Ayrton Senna and Alain Prost it is necessary to understand the personal characteristics that are prerequisite for a driver to rise above his peers in the modern era. Well-placed to provide such insights is Frank Williams, whose drivers have included six World Champions. One of them was Prost and while Senna only raced three times for the team before he was killed, Williams believes their shared traits meant their adversity was always going to be a case of an irresistible force meeting an immovable object.

'All the top drivers are difficult people with complex personalities,' Williams says. 'Ayrton was the best driver we ever had, but also the most demanding. He set himself the highest standards and pushed everybody around him to achieve those standards. Alain was different, but equally difficult to deal with. I wouldn't go so far as to say that

nice guys finish last, but the best Grand Prix drivers are driven, motivated, pushy, won't-accept-second-best, immensely competitive people. This is what makes them so good, because they're such bastards!'

When two such 'bastards' meet head-on in the same team friction, if not downright animosity, seemed inevitable. Compounding this potentially volatile situation was the fact that F1 team-mates are also the greatest rivals because the disparity of equipment dictates that the only true measure of respective talents can be made

when two drivers compete in identical cars.

Thus, in 1988, when Senna became Prost's team-mate at McLaren the stage was set for a major confrontation. Adding another dimension to their anticipated struggle for supremacy was the prospect of the ambitiously ascendant newcomer seeking to topple the established superstar from his perch - a syndrome that has always been a fascinating feature of the desperately competitive arena that is F1 racing.

Prior to their coming together at McLaren Prost had won 26 races and the 1985 and

meets
irresistible force

1986 driving titles, both with McLaren. Senna, five years his junior, had won six races in a Lotus and was obviously destined for greatness. Yet they had seldom met in wheel-to-wheel battles on the track and when they became team-mates they were surely on a collision course.

Both drivers hated to lose. As Keke Rosberg (the 1982 World Champion in a Williams) once famously said: 'Show me a good loser and I'll show you a loser. Period.' And when their team-mate represented an impediment to winning, or

worse still, had the potential to turn them into a loser, it was vital for Prost and Senna to take immediate steps to gain the upper hand at McLaren.

After simmering quietly during most of 1988 their mutual dislike ultimately boiled over at the 13th round, in Portugal, where Senna seemed to swerve deliberately in front of Prost, squeezing him so close to the Estoril pit wall that several signalling crews ducked for cover. Prost, who had been leading Senna at the time and went on to win, was livid, saying to Senna: 'If you want

the championship badly enough to die for it, you are welcome to it.'

Senna won that 1988 championship and Prost was second but the Frenchman's belief that his Brazilian team-mate was a dangerously disturbed madman accelerated when Senna revealed that he had found religion. 'Ayrton has a small problem,' said Prost. 'He thinks he can't kill himself because he believes in God, and I think that's very dangerous for the other drivers.'

Sensationalist elements of the F1 media eagerly seized on this and reported that Senna thought he was invincible because God was his co-pilot. 'It's unreal to say those things,' Senna responded angrily. 'Of course I can get hurt or killed in a racing car as anybody can and this feeling - this knowledge - is absolutely necessary for self-preservation.'

Feud-wise, their 1989 season got off to a flying start at the San Marino Grand Prix when Senna, who won the race, overtook Prost at the start. This manoeuvre, said a disgusted Prost, represented a sneaky breach of a previous agreement, instigated by Senna, that whoever was in the lead going into the first corner should be allowed to maintain it to avoid unnecessary risks.

Though Prost let Senna by on that occasion his open-door policy was most emphatically not in effect during the Japanese Grand Prix, where he clinched the championship after a collision between the two McLarens. They crashed on the entry to the Suzuka chicane, where Senna's attempt to overtake Prost was met by a hard right turn of the Frenchman's steering wheel. Prost walked away from his car (which was later found to be undamaged) and though Senna recovered and went on to win the race he was later disqualified (for receiving a push start) and Prost was declared the champion.

'I was absolutely sure,' Prost said after the Japanese race, 'that I would win or have an accident like this. The problem with Ayrton is that he can't accept not to win, and he can't accept that somebody might resist an overtaking move. A lot of times, both last year and this, I opened the door for him, and if I had not done it we would have crashed. I said before the race if this happened I would not open the door. And it happened.'

And it happened again the next year, and again at Suzuka, where Prost, now driving for Ferrari (having left McLaren largely because of Senna's presence), again closed

the door on Senna and the Brazilian again decided to use his McLaren as a battering ram to open it. The incident, in the first corner on the first lap, put both drivers out of the Japanese Grand Prix but Senna's lead over Prost in the standings meant the 1990 championship went to Senna.

'I am at peace with myself,' the Brazilian said afterwards, while the incensed Frenchman thought his actions were, 'deliberate, unsporting and intimidatory.'

Speaking a year later, after he had won the 1991 driving title (also at Suzuka), Senna

gave his version of what happened. 'It was a sad championship, but this was a result of the 1989 championship. Remember, I won that race and it was taken away. I was so frustrated that I promised myself that I would go for it in the first corner. Regardless of the consequences, I would go for it. He just had to let me through. I didn't care if we crashed. He took a chance, he turned, and we crashed. But what happened was a result of '89. It was built up. It was unavoidable. It had to happen. I did contribute to it, yes. But it was not my responsibility.'

According to Prost, Senna was responsible for more, 'dangerous and stupid behaviour,' perpetrated

against himself in the 1991 German Grand Prix. His inflammatory remarks (made on French television and which later resulted in Prost being given a suspended one race ban) included an accusation that Senna was deliberately, 'weaving across in front of me, braking suddenly and behaving in a strange way. If he ever tries that again I will push him off - for sure.'

Mercifully, their cars were rarely in close proximity again and the last time they met on the track was in the 1993 Australian Grand Prix at Adelaide. It was a momentous event for Prost who, now driving for Williams, had already clinched the championship (his fourth) and made his decision to retire from the sport, and for Senna, who would next year replace Prost at Williams after six seasons at McLaren.

In the race Senna scored his 41st (and sadly, his last) F1 victory, a record second only to the man who stood beside him on the victory podium in Adelaide. Prost finished second in his final Grand Prix, and would thus retire with 51 wins, making him the most successful of all F1 drivers.

Then, another kind of history was made as the two protagonists who had dominated the sport for so

long gave in to their emotions. Their deeply felt sense of occasion also moved them to overcome their mutual animosity and stage a dramatic and emotional post-race reconciliation. Prost extended a hand of friendship to Senna, a gesture which seemed to sweep away all those years of bitterness. A misty-eyed Senna hauled Prost up on to the top step of the podium to share the limelight and embraced him warmly. Their peace pact was sealed with champagne, which they playfully showered over each other before discussing their feelings.

Senna was asked what he really thought of his rival now that their celebrated feud was relegated to racing history. 'I think our attitude on the podium speaks for itself,' Senna said. 'It reflected my feeling, and I believe his feeling too.'

And did Prost think they could ever become close friends? 'I think only life will tell that. If you want to speak about the future you must also speak about the past and we don't want to do that. It's best that we remember only the good times we had.'

Tragically, Senna's future was short-lived, and few felt more badly about that than Prost. Just prior to the ill-fated 1994 San Marino Grand Prix at Imola Prost, now a temporary member of the media, and Senna met privately and agreed formally to end their five year feud. Prost said: 'We had the warmest conversation I can ever remember. For the first time I felt he really wanted to be friends.'

A few minutes later Alain Prost was one of millions of people who wept when Ayrton Senna was killed.

The Portuguese Grand Prix in 1988 (above) brought matters to a head after Senna lost his lead to Prost on the pit straight, but there were times when they could get along in public (below).

The Top 10 Drivers

Joe Saward

1. Ayrton Senna & Alain Prost

Twenty years from now F1 fans will look back at the late Eighties as an era when two enormous talents - Alain Prost and Ayrton Senna - met head-on. The fact that their careers were so intertwined makes it almost impossible to talk of one without the other.

Senna was the Latin with a tendency to flare up, Prost was The Professor, thinking before every act. Senna was explosive, Prost inexorable. It showed in their driving: Senna was the ace qualifier and big risk taker; Prost collected fastest laps and race wins.

It is always difficult to put drivers into historical perspective but the Senna/Prost rivalry will probably be compared in time to that of Tazio Nuvolari and Achille Varzi in the Thirties. The difference was that in the Eighties the sport had changed and had created a world where drivers could rarely be friends. F1 had grown so much that the pressure to win was intense and while the stars grew rich beyond their wildest dreams, they were forced to live in a rarefied world, which often created a sense of paranoia. Prost and Senna both suffered from this and it fuelled their rivalry. Once, in Hungary, they talked

for a long time and realised that they were very alike. But this entente could not survive their aggression on the track.

In an age where winning was everything and the paddocks of F1 were full of people who were not trustworthy, drivers had to be sharp and ruthless to make it. Both Senna and Prost proved that they were willing to do what was necessary. Winning was not just about being fast, it was about having the right car.

The darker sides of both men has too often been allowed to submerge the good sides of their characters. Both did things which they later regretted. Both had fervent fans and bitter critics. In Adelaide in 1993 their competitive relationship ended on an upbeat and dignified note. Too often they had not behaved like champions. In the end, both proved worthy of the accolade.

3. Nelson Piquet

The two Titans overshadowed their rivals in the Eighties to a great extent. The only man who ever really came close was Nelson Piquet, who won three World Championships and 23 Grands Prix. Nelson was full of guile and cunning and after finishing runner-up to Alan Jones in 1980 - the Australian surviving an attempt by the Brazilian to drive him off the track - Nelson outpsyched Carlos Reutemann in Las Vegas in 1981 to win his first crown. He then took a gamble and stayed loyal to Brabham during a difficult period in which it developed BMW turbocharged engines. This loyalty was paid off with another title in 1983. Nelson was probably too loyal to Brabham. He stayed two more years - and did not win much - before moving to Williams where he was once again a frontrunner. He might have won the 1986 title if Williams had run team orders, but instead Nelson and Nigel Mansell took points from each other and allowed Prost to sneak through to win. The following year Nelson made no such mistakes and although Mansell outdrove him on occasion, he won the title. His switch to Lotus in 1988 was a disaster and his career slipped after that.

4. Nigel Mansell

Mansell was another major player in the Eighties but he made life difficult for himself. His hard climb to F1 had made him a prickly character, but after years of frustration he woould win the World Championship in 1992. But at his moment of glory Mansell refused all offers from Frank Williams and quit F1, stomping off to America to win the Indycar title in 1993. Williams took him back for a few races after Senna's death in 1994 and he won a fortunate victory in Adelaide, after Hill and Schumacher collided. It would have been the perfect moment to retire but Nigel did not. Williams chose David Coulthard for 1995 and Mansell went into an unholy alliance with McLaren, which lasted just a few races before they fell out with one another - as they were always going to do.

Mansell had great talent and fire as a driver but this was often overshadowed by a political clumsiness and lack of grace which set people against him. If he had been a more political animal like Senna, Prost or Piquet, he might well have won two or even three world titles.

5. Niki Lauda

Niki Lauda was another driver with guile and cunning. Having won two world titles in the Seventies his return to racing in 1982 heralded an impressive second career. Doubts that he was still quick enough were soon dispelled with a victory in his third race back, and he went on to finish fifth in the World Championship that year. His big year was 1984 when he and fellow McLaren driver Prost dominated the season. Prost won seven races to Lauda's five but Niki was the more consistent, and won the title by half a point. In 1985 Prost had learned and was the dominant force. Lauda won in Holland but his retirement at the end of the year was well-timed.

6. Alan Jones

Alan Jones had more of the fire and determination of Senna. He had fought his way to the top without much money and won the Austrian GP in 1977 for Shadow, but it was not until he linked up with Frank Williams and Patrick Head in 1978 that real success came. The chemistry between the three worked brilliantly and the arrival of Head's marvellous Williams FW07 was the catalyst for a string of victories that not

only took Jones to the title in 1980 but also established Williams as a top F1 team. Alan was less happy in 1981, fighting team-mate Carlos Reutemann, but he retired with a victory in his final race at Las Vegas. Sadly, Jones was bored in retirement and an abortive comeback with Arrows in 1983 did little for his reputation and another with the Haas Lola team in 1985 was similarly disappointing.

7. Keke Rosberg

A driver in the same mould as Jones was Keke Rosberg, who took over at Williams when the Australian retired. The Finn had struggled to get a break in F1 and made the most of it when he became the Williams team leader at the start of 1982, as Reutemann decided it was time for him to retire as well. During that strange season when the

turbos were dominant but frail and when Ferrari lost both Gilles Villeneuve and Didier Pironi, Rosberg raced consistently. He won only once but it was enough to win him the world crown. In 1983 the normally aspirated Williams was outpaced by the turbo cars but Rosberg won a brilliant victory at Monaco with a perfect strategy in a wet/dry race. The 1984 season was largely wasted as the team developed the Honda turbo engines but Rosberg's brilliance shone through again in Dallas where he won a remarkable race in 100-degree heat.

He battled with Mansell for supremacy within the team in 1985 - winning three victories to Mansell's two - and decided long before the Williams became the dominant force at the end of the season to join McLaren as a replacement for Lauda. He stayed only one season and was honest enough to recognise that Prost was faster. He wanted to go out in style, however, and was leading his final race in Adelaide when a tyre failed.

8. Gilles Villeneuve

Rosberg's spectacular style was reminiscent of another of the top 10 stars of the decade, Gilles Villeneuve. The French-Canadian was already an established star when the Eighties began but struggled until his death in May 1982 with cars which were not competitive. The Ferrari engines were powerful but the chassis were awful. Villeneuve was a man who never gave up and his victories at Monaco and in Spain in 1981 were both virtuoso performances from a truly great driver. Gilles did not care about the World Championship; winning races was what mattered, but not at all costs. In 1979 he let Jody Scheckter win the World Championship because Ferrari wanted him to, and he was honourable about team orders.

The 1982 season looked like being a great year for Ferrari. The team hired Harvey Postlethwaite to solve its chassis problems and the 126C2 was very competitive. At Imola Villeneuve was beaten by his team-mate Didier Pironi, although he maintained that the Frenchman had done it despite team orders and that he himself had not been fighting. Villeneuve was furious at Pironi's treachery and hadn't spoken to him again before he died two weeks later in a ghastly qualifying accident at Zolder.

9. Didier Pironi

There are many who would argue that Pironi does not deserve a place in the top 10 of the Eighties but there is little doubt that had he not been maimed later in 1982 he would have been that year's World Champion. Talented and ruthless, he cut his teeth at Tyrrell in 1978 and '79 alongside the veteran Patrick Depailler. He was poached by Ligier in 1980 and led several races, winning in Belgium and doing enough to attract the attention of Enzo Ferrari, who was looking for a replacement

for Jody Scheckter. Pironi struggled to compete with Villeneuve but was clawing closer in 1982 when the Canadian was killed. As Ferrari team leader Pironi seemd to flourish and his progress that summer was impressive. He was leading the World Championship when he drove into a cloud of spray at Hockenheim thinking there was only one car ahead of him. The Ferrari cartwheeled down the track as it hit Prost's hidden Renault, and Pironi suffered terrible leg injuries. He underwent a string of operations and never gave up hope of returning to F1, but died in a powerboat race in 1987 before he could make his comeback.

10. Gerhard Berger

Taking too many risks killed another man who might have been a great racing driver

had he lived. Stefan Bellof showed at Monaco in 1984 that he was a star in the making. Unfortunately, he was killed in a sportscar accident at Spa the following year.

Thus the final slot must therefore go to Gerhard Berger, who rose through the ranks from humble beginning with ATS in 1984 to become a Ferrari driver in 1987. He won impressive victories in Japan and Australia that year but 1988 was a disappointment as McLaren swept all before it.

In 1989 his season was disrupted by a terrible accident in the now infamous Tamburello corner at Imola and at the end of that year he moved across to replace Prost at McLaren. Taking on Senna was a brave move but Gerhard argued that if you never went up against the best you could never be the best. The relationship hardened him and softened Senna. Having learned from Ayrton he headed back to Ferrari in 1993, but the Italian team was again in parlous state and in 1996 he moved on to Benetton. Gerhard scored 10 victories in eight different seasons, showing that he could win in all different kinds of car. If only Senna had not been around, he might have touched greatness...

The return of pit stops

In 1982 a 'new' racing tactic was developed by the Brabham team. The cars started events on half-tanks of fuel. This meant that the teams could use softer tyres which would be replaced when the car was being refuelled at the half-distance point. In theory, although around half a minute would be lost in the pits, refuelling would gain the driver around a minute in the course of a race.

Brabham's first attempt at such a tactic was to be at the British GP at Brands Hatch in July 1982. The team went to Donington Park before the event to practice and rumours suggested that they could complete a stop in just 14s. The expectant crowds in Kent would never find out because the Brabhams were both out after nine laps. It was a similar story at Hockenheim but finally in Austria both Brabham men made their pit stops. At each, 13 Brabham crew members went to work on the car, with two on each wheel - one with a wheel gun and the other to move the old wheel out of the way. The fuel was blasted into the tanks by pressured hose. Once again both cars retired in Austria but Patrese had been well ahead of the field when his engine seized.

The Brabham team did not win a race with a pit stop that year but in 1983 most of the other teams joined in. In Brazil Williams decided to refuel Keke Rosberg at mid-race but some of the fuel spilled out and there was a fire. Rosberg jumped out of the car while the fire was put out and was then ordered back into the cockpit and to rejoin. He was later disqualified for being push-started.

In the same race Piquet scored the first win including a pit stop, being at rest for 18s in mid-race. With the tactic having been proven there was a rush among rivals to get all the necessary equipment together in time for the French GP, and Renault and Ferrari joined the refuellers. At Imola Alfa Romeo and Lotus jumped on the bandwagon.

There was no doubt that refuelling added a new and exciting tactical element to the racing. Not only was there the possibility that something would go wrong and the driver would be delayed during his stop, but there were also possibilities of bluff and counter-bluff. At Detroit that summer Brabham bluffed the opposition into thinking that Piquet would stop for fuel and tyres, but the Brazilian simply drove on

without stopping. He was only a few laps short of the finish when he suffered a puncture.

By mid-season FISA President Jean-Marie Balestre had already begun to make noises that that refuelling was far too dangerous for the confines of the F1 pitlane. Bernie Ecclestone argued that it added to the racing and if teams were professional about the job there would not be any fires. In the end caution won the day. The FISA banned refuelling and it would not return until 1994 when Balestre was long-gone and Ecclestone was able to convince the teams to accept that refuelling was possible without fires. Despite a serious conflagration in the Benetton pit at the German GP that season, it remains to this day and the safety record has otherwise been good.

The top five

Joe Saward

Adelaide 1986

The most dramatic race of the Eighties was the World Championship finale of 1986 on the streets of Adelaide, Australia. Millions of F1 fans across Europe stayed up in the small hours of Sunday, October 26, to watch a three-way fight for the title between Nigel Mansell, Alain Prost and Nelson Piquet. Mansell had 70 points, seven more than Piquet, but they were split by Prost with 64. The McLaren-TAG was no match for the Williams-Hondas - which lapped Prost at several races - but Alain had collected points while the Williams pair took them from each other.

Mansell took pole from Piquet but at the second corner Ayrton Senna forced his way into the lead. Piquet and Keke Rosberg's McLaren followed him past Mansell and on that first lap Piquet overtook the Lotus to take the lead. On the next lap Senna dropped behind Rosberg and on lap four behind Mansell. Two laps later Prost was also ahead of Senna.

On lap seven Rosberg overtook Piquet and began to build a lead while a little later Prost got ahead of Mansell and chased after Piquet. On lap 23 Nelson spun. Prost's hopes seemed to evaporate a few laps later when he had a puncture and had to pit. He was back in fourth again.

Piquet charged back from his spin, passing Mansell for second place on lap 44, but Prost closed on the two Williams driver and with 25 laps to go all three were running together.

On lap 63 the battle became one for the lead, when Rosberg suffered a right rear tyre failure. Mansell was on course for the title when two laps later his left rear tyre exploded at 180 mph. He managed to avoid

As Prost abandons ship, Senna prepares for his sensational and controversial recovery, Suzuka 1989.

hitting anything but his championship hopes were over. Williams had no choice but to call Piquet to the pits and so Prost went into the lead. Piquet closed the gap from 15s to four but Prost won the race and the World Championship after a breathtakingly exciting race.

Suzuka 1989

Follow me: Villeneuve leads Laffite, Watson and Reutemann throughout the Spanish GP, Jarama 1981.

The 1989 Japanese Grand Prix is remembered as the race in which Alain Prost and Ayrton Senna collided. Victory went to Sandro Nannini in his Benetton. What is often forgotten is that Senna won the race on the road in stunning fashion.

Senna and Prost had gone to Suzuka with Alain 16 points ahead in the World Championship and only 20 more available. Senna had to win to keep his hopes alive. He took pole position but at the start Prost got away better and took the lead. For the first half of the race Prost chipped away to build a five second lead - and then Senna came back at him. By lap 40 they were only a second apart. Prost had the advantage on the straights, Senna was better in the corners.

races

The 1981 Spanish Grand Prix was Gilles Villeneuve's finest victory and a race of incredible tension. That year Ferrari had produced a powerful turbocharged engine but the 126CK chassis was so bad that Villeneuve himself described it as 'a hopeless fast red Cadillac'.

But it did not stop him trying to win races and in Monaco at the end of May he did just that, scoring Ferrari's first win for two years. Three weeks later the F1 circus rolled up at Jarama for the Spanish GP. Jacques Laffite took pole on his Ligier-Matra with the two Williams-DFVs of Alan Jones and Carlos Reutemann second and third ahead of John Watson's McLaren, Alain Prost's Renault and the Alfa Romeo of Bruno Giacomelli. Villeneuve was seventh.

Race day was incredibly hot and the temperature was around 100 degrees when the race began, with Jones and Reutemann blasting into the lead as Laffite made a poor start and Villeneuve scorched into third place at the first corner, snagging Prost's front wing as he did so. At the end of the first lap Villeneuve pulled out of Reutemann's slipstream and took second place. Jones quickly built a lead but on lap 14 - when he was around 10s ahead - he spun off.

This left Villeneuve with Reutemann on his tail. Behind them Watson, Laffite and Elio de Angelis emerged from the hurly-burly and all began to close on the duelling leaders. Reutemann was having some trouble with his gearbox and when Laffite arrived behind him there was little Carlos could do to stop Jacques overtaking. The Argentine would later drop behind Watson as well as the five front-runners became a train of cars, nose-to-tail for the remainder of the race.

Villeneuve had the power to get away from his rivals on the straight but in the corners they were all over him. Time and time again Laffite pulled alongside as they emerged from a corner but the Ferrari would surge ahead as the horsepower kicked in. The five remained locked together right to the flag, crossing the line covered by just 1.24s to record the second closest race in the history of F1 at the time.

It had been a sensational drive by Villeneuve and even Enzo Ferrari was impressed. The day after the race Villeneuve's boss compared his driver to the legendary Tazio Nuvolari.

Nannini at the chicane to take the lead, and won the race.

But it was Nannini who appeared on the podium. Senna had been excluded for missing the chicane. McLaren appealed the decision but the FIA Court of Appeal not only upheld the decision but fined Senna $100,000 and gave him a suspended six month ban.

In the record books the win still belongs to Nannini but anyone who was there will remember it as one of Senna's greatest days. A day when, in equal machinery, the Titans of the Eighties went up against each other - and Senna won.

At the end of lap 46 Senna made his move at the chicane. Prost saw him coming and turned into his team-mate's path. The two interlocked McLarens slid up the chicane escape road. Prost, thinking the World Championship was over, climbed out. To separate the cars the marshals pushed Senna backwards on to the track. They put the car into a dangerous position and so had to push it forwards again. As they did so Senna bump-started the engine. He drove through the chicane and rejoined. The nose of his car was damaged and he had to pit but he rejoined only five seconds behind Nannini. Senna's chase was furious and merciless. On lap 50 he sliced past

There but for fortune; tyre failure steals Mansell's 1986 crown.

Osterreichring 1982

The 1982 Austrian Grand Prix came at a time when F1 desperately needed some good news. That year Gilles Villeneuve had been killed at Zolder and a few days before the Zeltweg race, World Championship leader Didier Pironi was grievously injured in an accident in practice at the German Grand Prix.

Being at high altitude the Zeltweg track gave the advantage to the turbocharged cars and thousands of Ferrari fans came north in the hope that Patrick Tambay, in the only Ferrari, would give them something to cheer about. But in qualifying there was no catching the Brabham-BMWs

of Nelson Piquet and Riccardo Patrese. Behind came the two turbo Renaults of Alain Prost and Rene Arnoux, split by Tambay. The first of the normally aspirated cars was Keke Rosberg's Williams.

Ferrari's hopes were wiped out at the end of the first lap when Tambay picked up a puncture from wreckage from a first lap accident. This left the four turbos to pull away from the rest, with Patrese taking the lead from Piquet on the second lap. Lotus driver Elio de Angelis was driving a storming race in fifth, pulling well clear of the normally-aspirated opposition. And then things began to go wrong for the turbo men. Arnoux retired with engine trouble and when Piquet pitted for new tyres he was unable to pull away from fifth-placed Rosberg. Patrese pitted without losing the lead but three laps later his engine failed. Piquet was fading too and on lap 32 Rosberg moved into third place and began to chase down de Angelis.

On lap 49 Prost's Renault engine stopped. The normally aspirated battle became a battle for the lead. Neither man had won a Grand Prix and both were desperate to do so. Rosberg was quicker and the gap came down dramatically in the tense final laps. As they set off for the final lap Elio was 1.6s ahead. This was reduced to nothing by the time the pair came through the Texaco Schikane section and Rosberg was ready to challenge as they hurtled into the long sweeping Rindtkurve - the final corner.

But Rosberg lost momentum, having to brake behind the Lotus, and so de Angelis stayed ahead. On to the start-finish straight the Finn jinked out and tried to power past the Lotus, but he was still 0.050s behind when they crossed the line.

John Player Team Lotus had some close shaves. Colin Chapman (far right) was there to celebrate as de Angelis pipped Rosberg to the line in Austria in 1982 (above), while Senna repeated the feat at Jerez four years later (top and below).

Jerez 1986

It is hard to imagine a closer finish than the 1986 Spanish Grand Prix but there was one. At Monza in 1971 Peter Gethin and Ronnie Peterson crossed the finishing line, separated by only 0.010s. At Jerez 15 years later the gap between Ayrton Senna and Nigel Mansell was 0.014secs - the cars side by side as they crossed the line.

It was the culmination of a dramatic race which had involved several others cars. But in the early laps as those behind switched position, Senna stayed ahead. For 39 laps he was able to keep everyone at bay but then Nigel Mansell blasted ahead, his Honda engine clearly more powerful than the Renault in the back of Senna's Lotus.

Mansell pulled out a four second lead but Senna gradually reeled him in again, while Alain Prost sat on his tail in his McLaren-TAG. With 10 laps to go Senna challenged for the lead but Mansell held him off. Senna was not going to be beaten and tried again at the hairpin at the back of the track. This time he made it through and Mansell had to lift off, which allowed the canny Prost to sneak into second place.

Mansell decided to go for a desperate gamble. He pitted for fresh tyres, emerging 20s behind Senna with nine laps to go. And those were mighty laps as Mansell carved into Senna's lead at a rate of four seconds each time around. But ahead of him on the road was Prost - and surely he was not going to give up without a fight. But Mansell was able to pass Prost but was 0.7s slower on that lap than Senna. Mansell took up the chase again and as they set off on the last lap the pair were separated by only a second and a half. At the hairpin Mansell was right with Senna but there was nothing he could do through the next few corners. It was all going to be down to the acceleration out of the last corner. The Williams-Honda was quicker and as they crossed the line both men thought they had won the race.

Senna had...

> **'Mansell decided to go for a desperate gamble. He pitted for fresh tyres, emerging 20s behind Senna with nine laps to go'**

The dramatic success of Williams

Frank Williams struggled through the Seventies berated by his rivals as a hopeless failure. His racing teams were uncompetitive; he never had any money. Frank was simply surviving, waiting for the day when he could put all the elements together and build a winning team. He was probably the only one who really believed he could do it.

He joined forces with Patrick Head at the end of 1975 but an alliance with Canadian millionaire Walter Wolf was not a success and so Frank and Patrick went into business on their own in 1977. The team was put on its feet by John Makepeace, the manager of Barclays Bank in Didcot, who agreed to give Williams Grand Prix Engineering an overdraft of £30,000. That year they ran Patrick Neve in an old March 761. The Belgian brought £100,000 from Belle-Vue beer and this enabled the team to survive while Head and his small team designed and built the Williams FW06.

Commercial artist Tony Harris helped the team out when he was approached by the Saudia airline looking for someone to sponsor. Harris suggested Williams and the team received another £100,000. The problem was that none of the top drivers wanted to drive for Williams, but Alan Jones took a chance. He would run in second place six times that year and scored 11 points. At Monaco that year Saudia brought along a VIP guest called Mansour Ojjeh, owner of the TAG Group. He would become a major sponsor for the team in the years ahead.

As Head and his engineers worked on the FW07, Jones re-signed and it was expanded to a two-car operation with the recruitment of Clay Regazzoni. Unfortunately the new Williams FW07 was not ready for the start of the 1979 season and did not make its debut until the Spanish GP at Jarama on April 29 - the fifth race of the season. At the Belgian GP a fortnight later Jones qualified fourth but retired, and in Monaco Regazzoni finished the race just half a second behind the winner Jody Scheckter. At the French GP they were fourth and sixth.

The team planned to introduce some aerodynamic changes for Silverstone and in a matter of days the FW07 was transformed into a winning car. Jones took pole position and led the first 38 laps of the race before he was forced to retire with a water pump failure. And so, ironically, it was left to Regazzoni to give the team its first victory.

Jones was not down for long. He won the next three races in Germany, Austria and Holland and added a fourth victory in Canada in September to finish third in the World Championship.

That winter Carlos Reutemann was signed to partner Jones and in 1980 Williams was dominant. Jones won in Argentina, France, Britain, Canada and the United States; Reutemann won at Monaco and scored consistently. They finished first and third in the World Championship and Williams won its first Constructors' title.

The team has never looked back...

76

Personalities

Frank Williams

Frank Williams is an odd man - but you can understand why. He has been confined to a wheelchair and has needed round-the-clock nursing since he was paralysed in a road accident in March 1986. The focus of his life is his racing team. He thinks about it night and day and knows just how fragile success can be.

There was a time in the Seventies when Williams was the laughing stock of the F1 paddock. Every project in which he was involved was a disaster but he struggled on, refusing to be beaten.

So often in F1 the great teams are made up of a great wheeler-dealer and a great engineer and in 1975 Williams found the man he needed. Patrick Head had had enough of motor racing and was building his own boat. His efforts to build competitive racing cars in Formula 1, Formula 2 and Formula 5000 had not been entirely successful. Williams convinced him to try again and gave him 30 percent of a new company called Williams Grand Prix Engineering. The pair acquired an old carpet warehouse in Didcot in 1977 and success came two years later with the remarkable FW07 design which was driven to victories in 1979 by Alan Jones and Clay Regazzoni.

The team dominated the World Championship in 1980 and was in the running in 1981 - although its drivers Jones and Carlos Reutemann did not help one another in the points battle. Unusual management of drivers became something of a Williams tradition. Frank avoided team orders and let the drivers sort it out for themselves.

Clockwise from bottom left: John Barnard; Jean-Marie Balestre; Ron Dennis; Bernie Ecclestone. Frank Williams at centre, and inset with Patrick Head and Williams FW06.

Lauda and Ecclestone, old working partners.

Keke Rosberg won the 1982 World Championship and then Williams launched into a relationship with Honda which was to fund a great leap forward in the team's industrial infrastructure and a move to a bigger and better factory with its own wind tunnel. After a couple of difficult seasons Williams became the dominant force in F1 again, though with Williams in hospital for most of 1986 Nigel Mansell and Nelson Piquet let the Drivers' World Championship slip through their fingers.

Williams re-established his control of the racing team in 1987 but, by then, Ron Dennis had convinced Honda that McLaren was a better long-term bet. For the 1988 season Williams struggled with Judd engines while Frank negotiated a new relationship with Renault. Nine years later - with nine World Championships (four Drivers' and five Constructors') in the bag - that relationship is now coming to an end and Frank is looking to build a Williams-BMW package to take the team into a fourth phase of success in the 21st century.

When it comes to success Frank is ruthless. His attitude towards drivers upsets the team's fans. But Frank does not care. There is no sentiment involved. World Champions demand more money than he is willing to pay. If they lower their price - as Prost and Senna did - they can join the team but if none of the big names are available Frank and Patrick are quite happy to create new stars. They hire cheap youngsters and invest the money saved in research and development.

And that means that the team maintains a technical advantage over the opposition...

Bernie Ecclestone

People usually refer to Bernie Ecclestone as, 'the boss of Formula 1 racing,' and there is not a great deal which goes on in the paddock that Ecclestone does not know about. He is respected for his abilities as a dealmaker, a talent which has made him, the FIA and most of the F1 circus, very wealthy indeed. The ability to put together deals has given Ecclestone enormous power in F1 and he has been the dominant political figure in Grand Prix racing since the mid-Eighties,

maintaining a low profile until recent years when his accumulated wealth made him a public figure.

Ecclestone has always been controversial. Born in October 1930 he left school and worked as a laboratory technician while competing in scrambling and grass track events. He went on to road racing before trying his hand at car racing in a 500 cc Formula 3 Cooper. For three years he was a regular F3 racer but in September 1951 had a big accident at Brands Hatch and decided to retire and concentrate on building up his other businesses. The best of these was a motorcycle and car distribution operation, which he started in his parents' home. He would later open another motorcycle dealership and go on to build an empire in cars and bikes, as well as moving into property. In the late Fifties he began managing driver Stuart Lewis-Evans and went on to buy the Connaught F1 cars for Tasman races in 1957. In 1958 Lewis-Evans switched to a Vanwall and Ecclestone himself tried unsuccessfully to qualify for the Monaco and British GPs. The death of Lewis-Evans at the end of that season ended his interest in F1 for several years until his friend Roy Salvadori, by then the team manager of the Cooper F1 team, introduced him to Jochen Rindt.

Ecclestone became Rindt's manager until the Austrian was killed in 1970. Around this time Jack Brabham retired from racing and left designer Ron Tauranac to run his company. Tauranac sought assistance from Ecclestone and a year later Bernie bought the company and set about rebuilding Brabham into a winning force. The team won Drivers' World Championships with Nelson Piquet in 1981 and 1983 but under Ecclestone never managed to win the Constructors' title.

In the mid-Seventies Ecclestone became the leading light in the Formula One Constructors' Association and he and fellow team owner Max Mosley led their fellows in the fight over television rights with the governing body, headed after 1978 by Jean-Marie Balestre. The resulting battle was known as the FISA-FOCA War and was settled in March 1981 with the signing of the first Concorde Agreement. Ecclestone continued as head of Brabham, while also negotiating on behalf of FOCA until 1987 when he was appointed FIA Vice-President (Promotional Affairs). He remained head of FOCA but as the deals grew bigger the other team owners became less willing to take risks promoting races and so Ecclestone established a company called Formula 1 Promotions and Administration - which he owned solely - to do it on their behalf.

There is no question that Ecclestone masterminded the boom in interest in F1 in the late Eighties and early Nineties and he remains the powerhouse behind the sport, despite the fact that he is now 67 years old.

John Barnard

He is not always easy to work with; his cars do not always win first time out, but John Barnard remains one of the most sought-after engineers in Grand Prix racing.

In an era when rule changes made innovation increasingly difficult 'JB' masterminded two of the major technical breakthroughs of the Eighties: the all-carbonfibre monocoque in 1981 and the electronically controlled gearbox in 1989.

Barnard was trained in the no-nonsense school of engineering at Lola in late Sixties - he was a contemporary of Patrick Head with the Huntingdon company - and went on to work under Gordon Coppuck at McLaren. He designed briefly for Parnelli before being hired by Chaparral. He produced the ground-breaking Chaparral 2K, which won the 1980 Indianapolis 500.

At the time Ron Dennis of Project Four Racing was trying to put together an F1 team and was looking for a designer to produce a prototype chassis. Barnard suggested a radical chassis, built entirely from composite materials. Dennis took a risk and funded the development programme. In 1980, at the instigation of Marlboro, McLaren International was formed by a merger between Team McLaren and Project Four. Barnard's secret car became the McLaren MP4/1.

It was to be the basis of an entire family of successful F1 McLarens throughout the Eighties. The team won three consecutive

Graduates from Lola: Head and Barnard.

Drivers' Championships in 1984-85-86 but in 1987 Barnard was lured away to Ferrari with the promise of vast income and his own design centre close to his house in England. From there he masterminded the design of the Ferrari 640 with its revolutionary semi-automatic gearbox. This car won first time out in Brazil in 1989 and its successor enabled Alain Prost to challenge for the World Championship in 1990.

By then Barnard had been head-hunted to produce the Benetton-Ford B191. His greatest asset to a team is the understanding of what it takes to be successful in F1 and he remains one of the few men capable of putting together the industrial infrastructure needed. He is stubborn enough not to compromise on what is required and at Benetton this proved to be too much. The team management was unwilling to invest enough and so Barnard moved on, although the basic B191 design was carried forward by others to produce the B194 and B195 which Michael Schumacher drove with such success. The same basic design later became the Ligier JS43 and Olivier

Panis drove one of the cars to victory in Monaco in 1996.

John went on to work on a secret F1 project for TOM'S Toyota until the summer of 1992 when he was hired once again by Ferrari, but the arrival of Jean Todt - and his desire to have the whole Ferrari operation concentrated in Italy - meant that Barnard's new technical centre in England was gradually pushed aside. When his five-year contract with the Italians ended in early 1997 Barnard was snapped up by Tom Walkinshaw and is currently building up the Arrows technical team at Leafield.

Barnard admits that he is not happy unless things are being done his way, but experience has proved that more often than not the Barnard way is the right way...

Jean-Marie Balestre

The controversial head of the governing body of world motorsport between 1978 and 1991, Jean-Marie Balestre was a major figure in F1 racing in the Eighties.

He had a colourful background. He worked undercover for the French Resistance - posing as a member of the French Waffen SS. This led to confusion when he returned to France after the war but he somehow managed to convince the authorities of his story - although he has often had to go to court to defend himself since then - and was eventually awarded resistance decorations.

In 1950 he founded the magazine Autojournal with a friend, Robert Hersant, and the two built an impressive publishing empire. Balestre was a keen motorsport fanatic and in 1959 he founded the French

---

Caesar's Palace. F1's worst venue?

Some say that the Eighties was the decade in which the World Championship lost many of its great racing circuits. And there is no doubt that as safety issues became more important a lot of the great old corners were lost either because they were too simply dangerous to survive or because the organisers could not afford the money necessary to make the necessary changes. Money was an important issue in the changes during the decade as many of the organisers could not afford to meet the financial demands of the F1 circus.

The wonderful old Kyalami circuit in South Africa was the victim of politics, as the system in country at the time meant that some of the companies involved in F1 did not want to be seen going to South Africa. The circuit was sold and later altered to fit the idea of what racing circuits had to be in the Nineties.

It was a similar story with Buenos Aires which went out of the F1 calendar with the retirement of Carlos Reutemann and the onset of the Falklands War. It too would later be rebuilt, a shorter and less challenging place. Zandvoort disappeared in

The changing circuits

1986 because of environmentalists, and the Osterreichring fell victim to uncooperative local farmers.

Watkins Glen was dumped by the F1 fraternity because it was too remote and as the circus grew could not cope with the numbers of people involved, while Long Beach promoter Chris Pook called Ecclestone's bluff and switched to Indycar racing because the Americans offered them a better deal.

Jarama, a track most drivers enjoyed (but which had been derided as Mickey Mouse when it opened in 1967), fell victim to regional politics in Spain. It was a similar story in Brazil where the magnificent old Interlagos disappeared because Nelson Piquet came from Rio de Janeiro. The race moved to Jacarepagua and it was only when Sao Paulo's favourite son, Senna, was at his peak that Interlagos was revived, emasculated and put back into the World Championship.

Monza, Monte Carlo, Silverstone and Imola remained pretty much unchanged - chicanes were added - while Paul Ricard was chopped in two by safety inspectors after the death in 1986 of Elio de Angelis while testing at the track.

But the Eighties were not all bad news - except in America where the F1 circus wandered hopelessly from one soulless street circuit to another, visiting Detroit, Dallas and then Phoenix and trying hard to make it in New York. Tackiest of them all were the two races held round a parking lot at Caesar's Palace in Las Vegas.

The good news was that the World Championship regained Spa, one of its great circuits in the Sixties. Admittedly it was a.

shortened version of the original but it retained the spirit and the fast flow of the old track and the drivers loved it. The Germans tried to resurrect the Nurburgring but F1 did not much like it and commercial disputes led to Hockenheim becoming the German GP's permanent home.

Estoril was greeted with enthusiasm and Suzuka quickly won a place on the F1 calendar, while Adelaide arrived to provide a really quick street circuit, a great challenge and exciting races. Mexico City was also a good track though few professed to enjoying visiting the city itself.

Towards the end of the decade, however, there came a new kind of track developed, it seemed, for television. These were typified by Jerez and the Hungaroring, which proved to be forerunners of the drab new circuits of the Nineties.

Monaco: Unchanging throwback.

national karting authority. He would later establish the International Karting Commission. In 1968 he became secretary-general of the French national motorsport authority - the FFSA. He became its president in 1973. Frustrated that the FIA top management had little interest in motorsport he proposed the foundation in 1978 of the FISA, a sporting authority independent of the FIA. He became its founding president and for the next five years battled with Bernie Ecclestone and Max Mosley for control of F1. The so-called FISA-FOCA War ended in a compromise - known as the Concorde Agreement - which guaranteed that the FIA would get considerable revenue from the sale of F1's television rights, but these would be marketed by Ecclestone and FOCA. The money generated impressed the FIA and in 1987 Balestre became President of that organisation as well.

Despite a tendency to be bombastic, egocentric and controversial, Balestre's love of motorsport was not in question although his handling of the politics of the job was often clumsy. He banned ground-effect and turbocharging from F1 because the cars had to be slowed down, and he cancelled Group B rallying with immediate effect after the death of Henri Toivonen. His policies were never overturned, despite considerable opposition.

By the late Eighties, however, there were increasing question marks over his handling of important issues, notably the Senna-Prost collision at Suzuka in 1989. This led a furious Ayrton Senna to accuse him of manipulating the World Championship in favour of Frenchman Prost.

Despite his weaknesses, Balestre's control of the FISA and the FIA was unchallenged until 1991 when Max Mosley carried out a quiet campaign to win votes from smaller clubs all over the world rather than relying on the support of the big European bodies. Balestre was outmanoeuvred and defeated by 43 votes to 29.

By that time he was 70 years of age and had had a number of heart operations. His defeat in the FISA election marked the beginning of the end for J-MB and, although he remained FIA President until 1993, he did not oppose Mosley's 1993 plan to merge the FIA and the FISA into one organisation. In fact Balestre gave Mosley his support and, in exchange, was named President of the FIA Senate.

Ron Dennis

In the early Eighties ambitious team owner Ron Dennis put together an extraordinarily successful F1 package, based on his ability to convince big players to join his team and on the technical brilliance of designer John Barnard.

When Dennis left school in Woking at the age of 16 he probably never dreamed of the success and wealth that he would find in F1. He started out as an apprentice

mechanic and through a series of company takeovers was transferred to the Cooper Car Company, where he worked on the production line before becoming an F1 mechanic with Jochen Rindt. He was 18. In 1968 he went with Rindt to Brabham but then transferred to work with team boss Jack Brabham. Dennis stayed with the team until Jack retired at the end of 1970.

He and fellow Brabham mechanic Neil Trundle then established Rondel Racing and, using Brabham F2 cars, became a prominent force in that series in 1971 and 1972. They commissioned the design of a Grand Prix car - which was later sold and raced by Tom Pryce and others as the Token - but the oil crisis left the team without money and it had to fold. Dennis moved on to found a series of teams culminating in Project Four Racing, which ran a successful Marlboro-backed F2 team. It was the Marlboro link that led to a merger between McLaren Racing and Project 4 in 1980. McLaren

Ron Dennis

International was born and Barnard produced F1's first carbonfibre chassis - the MP4/1. The car was very successful, taking John Watson to second place in the 1982 World Championship, but Dennis knew that he needed a turbocharged engine and successfully convinced Williams sponsor TAG to buy into the company and to fund a Porsche-designed turbo V6. Dennis was also able to lure Niki Lauda out of retirement to lead the team. Alain Prost joined at the end of 1983 and the McLaren-TAG combination became one of the most formidable forces in motor racing history in 1984, winning a record 12 races. Lauda won the Drivers' title. Prost followed suit in 1985 and 1986.

Dennis lost Barnard in 1987 but was able to sign deals with both Honda and F1's rising star Ayrton Senna to create another outstandingly successful package. In 1988 the team won an incredible 15 of the 16 races. Prost won a third title but the following year was overshadowed by Senna and quit to join Ferrari. Senna was at the height of his powers in 1990 and 1991 and won both titles despite the increasing competitiveness of the opposition. By 1992 the Williams-Renault was the dominant force and Honda decided to withdraw. The move seemed to catch Dennis by surprise - he was by then a multi-millionaire, running the entire TAG/McLaren empire and building the amazing McLaren road car - and there followed a frustrating year with Ford, after which Senna left the team. Dennis dallied with Chrysler and Peugeot before getting a deal with Mercedes-Benz.

Much was expected from the new alliance but after two years there was little sign of progress and even Marlboro - Dennis's staunchest supporter - left the team. So far Mercedes and Marlboro's replacement, West, has stood behind Dennis and in 1997 there are signs of improvement. It now remains to be seen whether Dennis can lead McLaren back to the heady success it enjoyed in the Eighties.

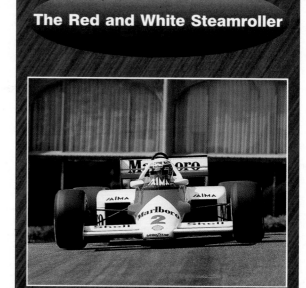

The Red and White Steamroller

In 1987, as the McLaren-TAG package began to struggle against the Williams-Hondas, McLaren's ambitious boss was already looking ahead for an engine to replace the TAG turbo and trying to convince Honda that his team would be more successful than Williams. At the same time he was working to convince Lotus driver Ayrton Senna that he would be much more successful at McLaren.

With Marlboro paying the bills, Dennis was able to put two F1 superstars, Alain Prost and Ayrton Senna, into identical cars. The chassis was a reworked version of John Barnard's successful cars of the early Eighties, produced by a team of engineers led by Steve Nichols.

With only one year left for the turbocharged engines - F1 went normally aspirated in 1989 - Honda decided to concentrate on the turbo engines, rather than switching to a new V10. The resulting package - the McLaren-Honda MP4/4 - was remarkable. When it appeared in March 1988 it immediately set sensational lap times at Imola, Senna lapping two full seconds faster than Gerhard Berger's Ferrari. At the Brazilian Grand Prix at the beginning of April Prost beat Berger to victory. A month later at Imola Senna led home Prost. Prost struck back, winning Monaco and Mexico but then Senna won Canada and Detroit.

The competition was left stunned. There was nothing they could do to challenge the might McLaren-Hondas. However impressive it may be, domination in F1 is never good to watch and the F1 circus yawned its way through that summer, hoping that something would break the brilliant monotony. It happened only once, at Monza in September. Senna led 49 of the 51 laps but at the first chicane on the penultimate lap he stumbled while trying to lap F1 debutant Jean-Louis Schlesser, standing in for Nigel Mansell at Williams. The Frenchman did everything he could to stay out of Senna's way but somehow the two collided. Way behind, Gerhard Berger took the lead and led home a Ferrari 1-2 finish amid scenes of unrestrained excitement.

But after Monza the winning machine was back on the rails again. When they headed out to Japan Senna had seven wins to his name, Prost six. Although Alain was ahead overall the scoring system meant that only the best 11 scores could count. If Senna won at Suzuka the title would be his. Having taken pole position with Prost alongside him, the Brazilian stalled at the start. He was able to bump-start the car as it rolled down Suzuka's start straight. He was 13th as the field streamed into the first corner. At the end of that first lap he had made up five places and was eighth. Next time around he was sixth and with two more overtaking moves in two laps he was fourth. And then it began to rain and Senna, in his element, was utterly dominant. In five laps Senna reduced Prost's lead from 11secs to less than two. On lap 28 Senna overtook his team-mate and slowly pulled away to win. It had been a masterful performance - and the highlight of a remarkable season. The record books show that McLaren scored 15 wins, 15 pole positions and 10 1-2 finishes. These figures are never likely to be beaten...

http://www.F150.com

A theatre of controversy

Tony Dodgins

Push comes to shove: Prost and Senna at Suzuka in 1990 (left). Hakkinen (above) jumps in Adelaide for McLaren in 1994.

Grand Prix racing was dragged screaming into the Nineties against a backdrop of controversy as Ayrton Senna accused the governing body of rigging the World Championship after Alain Prost had run into him at Suzuka the previous October.

The saga ran and ran. All publicity is good publicity so they say, and it kept the sport in the news during the off season. Increasingly throughout the Nineties, F1 became theatre.

Senna apologised eventually but at the end of 1990 there was a re-run. This time Ayrton had Alain off, but at 150 mph instead of 45. There was widespread condemnation but, to Senna, it was an eye for an eye. We would see the theme repeated as the decade wore on.

The incident saw the third straight championship success for the daunting McLaren-Honda combination and Senna served up more of the same in 1991. But a subtle shift was underway. Nigel Mansell was back at Williams after two seasons at Ferrari and the FW14 was clearly the chassis of the year. Renault's superb RS3 V10 was also a match for Honda's V12. Mansell's early races were spoiled by problems with the new Williams semi-automatic gearbox but the writing was on the wall. The team had upped its game and although it didn't ultimately beat McLaren-Honda, technical director Patrick Head vowed to rectify the situation in 1992.

Throughout history you can pinpoint defining moments and 1992 was one such for Grand Prix racing. Williams perfected active suspension - simply put, computer-controlled ride height optimised the car's aerodynamics. Nelson Piquet used an active Williams at Monza in 1986 but development was slow. Ironically, Mansell was a strident critic after a couple of frights in 1988. Now though, he benefited enormously.

After much testing by Damon Hill, Williams committed to active. With the semi-automatic gearbox now augmented by traction control, Mansell enjoyed a huge performance advantage which carried him to the world title by the Hungarian Grand Prix in August.

Mansell did not acknowledge technical superiority too often, a fact which annoyed both team and observers, but it was all too obvious. In race one at Kyalami, Senna finished 35s behind. Asked what he thought about that, Ayrton's expression made words superfluous. But just in case anyone was left in any doubt, he said stonily: 'In equal equipment it doesn't happen like that...'

It was Max Mosley's first full season pulling the levers of power at the FIA. At first he said he was committed to allowing F1 to follow its technological course. Later though, he admitted he hadn't fully understood exactly how far things had gone. At Spa that year, Mansell himself said: 'Once we drop the clutch, the computer and the software will decide who has the best traction off the line.'

The art of gearchanging had also been taken away and now the start was governed by electronics. Things were going too far. Four-wheel steering was on

Max Mosley, the FIA's new broom.

the way and when McLaren launched the MP4/8 for 1993, team boss Ron Dennis acclaimed it the most sophisticated racing car of all time. It would not be too long, he said, before a car could do a lap of its own accord, sensing where it was on the circuit and acting accordingly.

Not only was the driver's contribution gradually being eroded, but soon F1 would become the ultimate white knuckle ride. Drivers would become five stone midgets with big neck muscles.

Politics is never far behind development in F1. While there was support for taking things back to basics, that idea did not curry favour among teams such as McLaren and Williams who had invested heavily in mastering the technology.

The FIA had a problem. The Concorde Agreement dictated that in order to make changes, unanimous agreement was needed among the teams. Benetton boss Flavio Briatore was a vocal detractor of that principle and there was an amusing incident when Williams shot itself in the foot by missing the entry deadline for the 1993 season by a single day. Unanimous agreement was needed to allow the team in and, surprise surprise, Mr Briatore did not play ball. Just making a point, he said...

Williams admitted to embarrassment at the consequence of sloppy office administration and there was a fair degree of mirth at the suggestion that if Frank agreed to a spot of technological regression, should we say, then he might even be allowed to play!

Unsurprisingly the FIA could not achieve unanimous agreement for a ban on driver aids and had to act in a more heavy-handed way. At Montreal in 1993 a bulletin from technical delegate Charlie Whiting declared that everyone bar Minardi was illegal. The active systems of others contravened the rule on moveable aerodynamic devices and traction control was unlawful because the rules said that drivers needed to be in control of their cars at all times. The FIA pointed out that it was perfectly within its rights to demand that everyone turn up in France without active suspension a couple of weeks later. But also that, if the major players could see their way to agreeing a driver aids ban for 1994, then they could do business.

Dennis, aggrieved, pointed out that it was nothing less than a blatant attempt to bring down the 'haves' to the level of the 'have nots.' Meanwhile Niki Lauda, a Ferrari adviser, supported the technology ban, adding that F1 had become 'so boring that viewers can't keep awake long enough to switch off their televisions!' Ferrari, of course, had more money than anyone. But, said the cynics, they hadn't mastered the technology. This was undeniable. When Gerhard Berger first tried Ferrari's active system at an Estoril test, he was seven seconds off the pace. More than that, Berger does not scare easily and yet his eyes were wider than a five-year-old's on Christmas morning.

The FIA pointed out that they could cancel all the control systems on safety grounds if they so desired. And that case was strengthened when Alessandro Zanardi suffered a Lotus active failure at Spa's daunting Eau Rouge and was extremely fortunate to survive.

'I don't remember a lot, but we had a yellow light in the car which came on if you had a pressure failure in the active system,' he explained. 'The problem is that at more than about 125 mph the pressure is very high. Not only does it have to hold the car up but it also has to cope with the downforce. I just had time to see the warning light come on and think: "Oh God, not here!" I went straight into the wall and I'm lucky to be able to talk about it.' Indeed he was.

Black Sunday: Imola 1994.

Irvine in the flames, Spa the same season.

For 1994 then, a ban on driver aids was pushed through. Active suspension, traction control, four-wheel steering - all were gone. Semi-automatic gearboxes stayed because they eliminated the expensive engine damage caused when drivers over-revved on a downchange.

Sadly, 1994 was to be another of those defining moments. When Ayrton Senna was killed at Imola on May 1, it was possibly the most high profile death since JFK. The shock waves transcending the sport brought to mind Jim Clark's fatal accident at Hockenheim on April 7 1968. Except that today we live in times of media saturation. The very moment of death of the world's most high profile sportsman beamed live into living rooms throughout the world, presented problems for F1.

The popular Roland Ratzenberger had died the previous day in circumstances just as tragic, but Senna was an icon. Brazil declared three days of national mourning. When Karl Wendlinger crashed in practice at Monte Carlo 10 days later and was hospitalised in a coma, Mosley knew he had to be seen to act. Questions were being raised at government level and so the FIA pushed through a range of technical changes to the cars, to be introduced in stages, which addressed safety issues by cutting downforce and reducing cornering speeds.

Predictably that led to further problems. To some team owners it was simply the FIA again trying to narrow the gap between the top teams and their pursuers. On the contrary, some argued, new regulations would actually magnify the gap because only the well heeled could properly accommodate the upheaval mid-season.

Benetton boss Flavio Briatore publicly criticised Mosley and said that the changes could not be done safely in the time

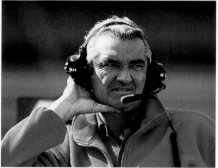
Flavio Briatore: colourful.

available. He told his drivers that they would race in the Spanish Grand Prix on their own and the FIA's responsibility. There was some sympathy for this. Diffuser changes demanded by the new regulations changed the forces acting on the rear of the car and led to wing failures in testing. Pedro Lamy's Lotus broke at Silverstone and the young Portuguese suffered badly broken legs.

And then there was Benetton. In the wake of Senna's death, Michael Schumacher was obviously heir apparent. Prior to the Imola tragedy Schumacher had won the opening two races. Senna had found the Williams FW16 difficult but was still surprised by the pace shown by Schumacher's Ford V8-powered Benetton. After the accident, a spell of Schumacher domination was expected as Hill adjusted to his new role as Williams team leader, but it was the French Grand Prix that set tongues wagging. Williams qualified 1-2, having brought Nigel Mansell back from America with Renault Francs and a donation (if that is the correct term!) from Bernie Ecclestone. Hill reckons he made his second best start of the season from pole but Schumacher streaked between the pair and disappeared. Rivals muttered about traction control, as Senna had.

Two weeks later at Silverstone, Schumacher committed the heinous crime of nosing ahead of pole man Hill on the parade lap. He should have been placed at the back of the grid but race officials allowed him to start from his grid position. He was then given a stop-go penalty but ignored it while the team argued. Finally the black flag appeared and he ignored that too. The FIA convened a special meeting of the World Motor Sport Council and banned him for two races. At the same time they said that Benetton was one of three teams found to have a computer system 'capable of breaching the regulations.'

The 'launch control' controversy and suspicions of traction control usage soured Benetton's success and there was further trouble when Schumacher's team-mate Jos Verstappen suffered a refuelling fire at Hockenheim. The controversial practice had been reintroduced to spice up the show, to general consternation, and such an eventuality was widely anticipated. The real problem came when the FIA inspected the team's refuelling apparatus back at base and found that a filter had been removed. The regulations specifically banned any modification to the equipment.

Popularity rules.

Would Benetton be removed from the championship perhaps? No. The team employed eminent QC George Carmen, the matter was blamed on a junior mechanic and quietly swept under the carpet. Schumacher served his two-race suspension and both races were won by Hill, but not before Michael had been disqualified from his win at Spa when the new underbody plank was discovered to infringe the permissible wear regulations.

When Hill also won in Suzuka it set-up up a championship showdown in Adelaide. Schumacher led by a point going to Australia and was two seconds clear of Hill's Williams when he ran wide and hit the wall on lap 36. Damon, who hadn't seen the impact, dived inside at the next corner, Michael turned in, contact was made and neither finished. Schumacher was champion. A year of tragedy and controversy was finally done.

But the sport's television ratings soared, a factor close to the heart of promotional impresario Bernie Ecclestone. He was about to invest millions in his global TV village to launch pay-per-view in F1. He could then increase revenue by selling the sport to both terrestrial and pay TV.

In order to score, however, Ecclestone has to make sure racing is entertaining enough to justify its existence in the television superleague. Keeping the viewing figures up keeps the sponsorship bucks rolling in.

Continued Schumacher/Hill rivalry was the backbone of the 1995 season, with Michael again coming out on top. When the German left Benetton for Ferrari, Hill finally achieved his ambition and took the

> **'..those who sought sport discovered it was ever harder to find.'**

title in 1996. But new team-mate Jacques Villeneuve took him right down to the wire.

Hill's reward was an Arrows drive for 1997 as Williams replaced him with Heinz-Harald Frentzen. Villeneuve started the season undisputed championship favourite but a series of errors, some down to the team and some to Jacques, allowed Schumacher and Ferrari to keep the championship battle alive right down to that memorable finale at Jerez.

A little help was needed along the way. There was a yellow flag incident which cost Schumacher five points in Austria when he had opened a decent lead, and the same for Villeneuve in Japan when he had done likewise.

The climax could not have been scripted better. Unbelievably, Villeneuve, Schumacher and Frentzen all recorded the same qualifying time down to the last thousandth and for 47 laps the championship protagonists fought it out head-to-head. Perhaps inevitably there was contact again. This time Schumacher lost out.

Just below the surface, Bernie Ecclestone's planned stock market flotation simmered away. For it to work effectively there had to be harmony. Ecclestone stood to make billions out of selling something which, dissident team owners argued, might not be his to sell. And if it was, they wanted a decent slice of the action. The dispute rumbled on.

Meanwhile, proposed tobacco advertising bans threatened to subdue F1's collective sponsorship pot by anything up to £200 million per year. Surely nothing a million or two in the right place couldn't sort...

The FIA's 50 year-old World Championship thunders on towards the Millennium apparently healthier than it has ever been. But is it sport, business, politics or entertainment? In the Nineties, it seems, it can be all things to all men. But those who sought sport discovered that it was ever harder to find.

●

Schuey at Benetton, 1995, arguably his least controversial and most successful season.

Overtaking, what overtaking?

Several factors have conspired to make overtaking in Grand Prix racing more and more difficult. The remarkable efficiency of F1 braking systems makes the biggest single impression on any driver sampling a Grand Prix car for the first time. And shrinking braking distances mean fewer opportunities to outbrake other drivers.

The aerodynamic development of cars is another major factor. Drivers repeatedly speak about the problems of running in disturbed air from the car in front. The front wing does not work as effectively, the car understeers and the driver has to come off the throttle. Overdo it and you go off.

Mika Hakkinen demonstrated the phenomenon as it affected him in the Parabolica at Estoril while he making his McLaren debut in 1993. 'I got it badly wrong. I had been testing for McLaren while Michael Andretti raced and was in a racing situation for the first time for a long while. I was following Alesi's Ferrari very closely. HisV12 was a noisy engine when you were following it. Pretty dirty also, spraying oil everywhere, but very powerful. It's hard enough anyway following closely, but our Ford V8 just wouldn't give me the opportunity to overtake him. He just disappeared on the straight.

'I was trying to go quicker and quicker around Parabolica, get a really good tow and then attack him at the end of the straight. This time I was round the corner a little quicker than him, catching, catching, catching. Alesi is a driver who is always on the limit and I was even more so. Coming out of the corner I was right on his tail. The flames from the Ferrari engine were touching my front wing! I went up on the kerb, got some understeer, but thought: 'This is it, I can get him now!' I knew that if I lifted I was going to lose everything. The whole car was on the kerb, I still didn't lift and the next moment I was on the grass. I still didn't lift but it was a big ditch...

'It was a big shunt. We're talking 160 mph plus and you don't have small accidents at that speed....'

Add in the additional grip from the softer rubber which arrived in 1997 courtesy of the tyre war and drivers were generating more decelerative g-force and spending less time on the brakes than ever before.

The FIA asked the F1 Technical Working Group for its recommendations to increase overtaking opportunities and the result was the new 'skinny car' regulations which came into operation for 1998. Narrower cars meant less area to generate downforce, the new grooved tyres meant less grip and a restriction on brake component materials was designed to increase the braking distance. A solution? Only time will be the judge.

The Top 10 Drivers

Tony Dodgins

1. Ayrton Senna

To some, the greatest racing driver of all time. To others, a man whose egocentricity fired a win at all costs attitude which flawed his genius. The old enemy was Alain Prost and their rivalry was the central theme of Grand Prix racing as the Eighties gave way to the Nineties.

In reality Senna never drove a car truly worthy of him this decade. McLaren thoroughness allied to Honda power and reliability gave him the 1991 championship against re-emerging Williams. Even Ayrton's ability could not hold a candle to Mansell in an active FW14B in 1992. Much to his chagrin, he couldn't handle Prost in the '93 Williams either, but five wins in a Ford-powered McLaren spoke volumes.

Two races that year epitomised Senna. The first was Donington. He had an instant feel for grip and that superb drive in the European Grand Prix showed it perfectly. And then there was Adelaide. In what he knew to be his last Grand Prix for McLaren and Prost's last race ever, he was determined to win. He drove flawlessly to end an era on top. He went from podium to stage, joining Tina Turner on stage at the end of season party for 'Simply the Best.' Fitting. Sixty-five pole positions said it all. The out and out quickest there has ever been?

2. Michael Schumacher

Like Senna, Schumacher possesses the same freakish ability to attune instantly to any surface. He also shares a similarly uncompromising attitude. From the moment he qualified seventh on his debut in a Jordan at Spa in 1991 it was obvious that he had talent to throw away.

He scored his first win one year on at the same majestic Ardennes circuit, matured as Benetton closed the gap to Williams in 1993 and emerged as the new king in the wake of that black day at Imola in May '94. He won the championship despite losing second place at Silverstone when he ignored a black flag, his Spa victory on a technicality and being banned from two races won by his chief rival.

Unfortunately, unproven allegations that Benetton used illegal traction or launch control systems, allied to the final round collision with Hill in Adelaide, shaded his achievement somewhat. Ultimately, if there were any doubts they were dispelled by the drubbing he handed Hill and Williams in 1995. The move to Ferrari did not stop him winning three times in 1996 and in 1997 he was magnificent. Until that 48th lap at Jerez, that is.

Races such as Barcelona '96 and Monaco '97 remind you so much of Senna and the great tragedy is that motor racing missed out on a few years of head-to-head rivalry between these two.

3. Alain Prost

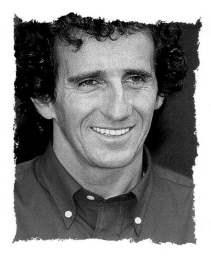

The record book says Alain Prost: 51 wins. You cannot argue against that and even if he was at his best in the mid-Eighties, Prost was still a mighty force during the three seasons he competed in this decade.

In 1990 he seized the initiative at Ferrari and overshadowed Nigel Mansell, spurred on by the burning desire to put one across Senna, McLaren and Honda after that acrimonious 1989 season. It all ended similarly, of course, with that infamous first corner shunt at Suzuka.

The following season's Ferrari was a truck by comparison and when Prost said as much he was promptly shown the door. He had an enforced sabbatical in '92 and took Mansell's place at Williams for '93. It was a great pity that Nigel didn't stay around to face him down, but as it was, Alain stroked to his fourth world title.

Caught with Prost at McLaren in 1984/85, Niki Lauda could not believe his qualifying pace, but Alain never looked quick. His style was neat, precise, classical. It was a total fallacy to say he couldn't drive in the rain. On one lap he was quicker than anyone bar Senna. It was just that driving blind into a wall of spray at 150 mph didn't square too well with acutely developed intelligence and instincts of self-preservation.

4. Nigel Mansell

Ironically, the full extent of Nigel Mansell's ability was not properly appreciated until he left F1. It was his ability to win the 1993 IndyCar title at the first time of asking, in unfamiliar surroundings, which really grabbed everyone's attention.

Yes, we'd all seen what he did in 1992 but it was behind the wheel of the only active chassis in the field. We'd also seen Prost drive him into premature retirement at Ferrari in 1990 and Mansell taking to the hills when it was obvious that Prost was going to be part of the Williams scene in '93. Mansell, however, contends that it wasn't a case of running, it was the team backing him into an untenable position.

In truth, Mansell deserved to be World Champion in 1986. That he finally achieved his goal was down to his greatest assets: sheer bloody-minded determination and competitiveness.

He possessed great car control, abnormal bravery and great strength. He always gave 100 percent and featured in some of the most memorable overtaking moves of recent time - Piquet at Silverstone in'87; Senna at Hungaroring in 1989; Berger in Mexico 1990. And then there was that qualifying lap at Silverstone in 1992. He set great store by being The People's Champion.

5. Damon Hill

Changes of fortune don't come much more dramatically than they did for Damon Hill. In 1992 he combined his Williams test work with the unenviable task of racing the underdeveloped, underfunded Brabham BT60. The following season Nigel Mansell's defection to IndyCars saw Hill projected into the limelight alongside Alain Prost in Grand Prix racing's best car.

Hill seized his chance. He won three times in his freshman year as Prost mopped up the championship. In 1994 he faced Senna but the tragedy at Imola unexpectedly thrust Hill into the role of Williams team leader.

Renault in particular showed a lack of confidence and helped to fund Mansell's return to Williams for the French Grand Prix. Damon saw him off and that did wonders for his confidence. Just as his father had helped Colin Chapman pick up the pieces after Jim Clark's death in 1968, so Damon now helped Frank Williams do likewise. He emerged as a genuine team leader and took Schumacher all the way to that controversial conclusion in Australia.

He suffered in 1995 when his machinery was superior to Schumacher's but still delivered - too late to save his drive - in 1996. Hill endured a miserable season at Arrows as reigning champion before attempting to revive his career at Jordan. His character, honour and natural dignity mark him as a man apart.

6. Jacques Villeneuve

Any driver who wins a championship largely based on equal equipment is worthy of much respect. Jacques Villeneuve showed pace, racing instinct and cool intelligence en route to the IndyCar title with Team Green in 1995. It was a passport to the best car in F1.

He took pole position on his Grand Prix debut in Melbourne and only an incident which provoked an oil leak prevented him winning the race. Ultimately though, he couldn't wrestle the initiative from Damon Hill throughout 1996 but managed to take the championship down to the wire, scoring four wins. His pass of Schumacher at Estoril stood out as one of the season's highlights.

In 1997 he had to cope with the pressure of starting the season as undisputed favourite. There were two wins in the opening three races but then came howlers at Monaco, Montreal and Magny-Cours. There was another mistake at Hockenheim and then the yellow flag incident in Japan. Too many errors to justify a championship? Perhaps, but Schumacher's antics in Spain swayed public sympathy and Villeneuve's vital pass was the move of the year. The man is a racer.

He doesn't just talk about 'going to the edge,' he does it. Intelligent and articulate when he wants to be, he's a free spirit and good news for F1.

7. Gerhard Berger

Never a genuine championship contender, Gerhard Berger has nonetheless always been a frontrunner in F1. Three years as McLaren team-mate to Ayrton Senna was a sobering experience and made him acutely aware of his position in the scheme of things, while doing less harm to his earning capacity than might have been expected.

Berger's second spell at Ferrari (1993-'95) did not begin well as the Scuderia struggled with evolving active technology. The ban on such things for 1994 came as something of a relief. He spent the last four years of his career as team-mate to Jean Alesi at Ferrari and then at Benetton.

Wins were not commonplace. He was handed Japan in 1991 by Senna, there were Canada and Australia in 1992, Germany in 1994 and then, emotionally, three years later a repeat performance for Benetton at Hockenheim in 1997. It was his best win and followed health problems, news that Benetton would not be keeping him and then the death of his father in a light aircraft accident. Berger handled himself admirably, as he did in the aftermath of Senna's accident, which probably affected him more deeply than any other driver. He was one of the sport's true gentlemen.

8. Jean Alesi

Jean Alesi burst on to the Grand Prix scene in 1989 with an electrifying performance at Paul Ricard in a Tyrrell. Then there was Phoenix the following year, when he held off Senna's McLaren for half the race and actually repassed the Brazilian momentarily, and then Monaco. He was the fashionable bright young thing and ended up with three contracts in his briefcase for 1991.

Sadly, Alesi's career has never fulfilled its promise with Canada 1995, the day of his 31st birthday, yielding his only win. His Latin temperament allied to the occasional preposterous act have given him an undeserved reputation for wildness. In fact he is one of the more solid, dependable drivers on the grid, with uncanny car control. These past two years, however, it has been masked somewhat by the nervous tendencies of the Benetton chassis.

You get the feeling that Jean's time has passed. With no disrespect to Sauber, 1998 was due to be his first season since 1991 in something other than a recognised front-running team.

9. Mika Hakkinen

For many, the second quickest man in Grand Prix racing today, behind Schumacher.

Hakkinen's junior record was superb, he jumped straight from Formula 3 into the Lotus team in 1991 and was then signed by McLaren for 1993. He had to sit out most of the year as

test driver while McLaren persevered with Michael Andretti. Senna, by this stage, had become a little disillusioned and was on his way to Williams for 1994 anyway. When Andretti quit after Monza and Hakkinen stepped in to outqualify Ayrton at Estoril, it really registered with the maestro and no doubt helped spark those mesmerising drives from him in Suzuka and Adelaide.

Ford, Peugeot and Mercedes/Ilmor engines in successive years did not do Hakkinen any favours and then came the near fatal accident at Adelaide in 1995. He worked wonders to get over the psychological effects of that and, as McLaren and Mercedes made progress in 1997, he emerged as a genuine threat. His maiden victory at Jerez may not have come about in the manner he would have wished, but it was long overdue. Something of an enigma, he can be monosyllabic or perceptively articulate depending on how the mood takes him.

10. Nelson Piquet

Undoubtedly, the best of Nelson Piquet belonged in the Eighties but there were some highlights in the Nineties too. After a couple of seasons in uncompetitive Lotuses, Flavio Briatore threw Piquet a lifeline in the form of a performance-related contract for 1990. While his retainer was relatively modest, it was apparently supplemented by $100,000 per championship point. Nelson scored 44 and did very nicely, thank you. He finished the season with back-to-back wins - very fortunate in Suzuka but the result of a sterling drive in Adelaide after Senna and Mansell had taken themselves out of contention.

With Pirelli rubber in 1991 it was hard to evaluate Piquet's performances but his position at Benetton was undermined by the arrival of both Michael Schumacher and Tom Walkinshaw, the latter having a commitment to Martin Brundle for 1992. Piquet, a three-time champion remember, found the novice German's pace difficult to live with. Outqualified every time, Piquet determined to turn the tables on Schumacher in Adelaide. To his great credit he achieved it - no mean feat as we have come to appreciate. He finished fourth in the 14-lap shortest Grand Prix on record, a race which also turned out to be his last.

Personalities

Max Mosley

Born in 1940, the younger son of Sir Oswald Mosley via his second marriage, to Diana Mitford, Max Rufus Mosley has been steeped in motor racing for well over 30 years.

At Oxford, Mosley became secretary of the Union and studied physics. He went on to specialise in patent and trademark law and was a practising barrister before he got himself seriously involved in motor racing. He raced up to Formula 2 level before becoming the 'M' in the acronymous nme of the newly founded March company (Mosley, Alan Rees, Graham Coaker and Robin Herd).

They didn't do things by halves. At the time March was founded, F1 was much more accessible. You could build a chassis, buy a Cosworth engine off the shelf and go racing. Mosley had met Herd at University and Robin had a reputation as one of the brightest up-and-coming young designers on the scene. The formation of March just happened to coincide with Matra deciding to run its own V12 engine in F1. Jackie Stewart, who had just won the world title for Ken Tyrrell in a Ford-powered Matra, didn't fancy the V12 and suddenly Tyrrell needed a chassis. Mosley and Herd thus began their first season as Grand Prix constructors with the reigning World Champion in the cockpit!

In the early days Mosley listened with some disbelief to the unstructured ramblings of the Grand Prix Constructors' and Entrants' Association and quickly determined to do something about it. A year or so later Ron Tauranac sold Brabham to Bernie Ecclestone and the pair soon got together. Rapidly they were doing everything for the GPCA, which spawned FOCA.

With Ecclestone's negotiating skills and Mosley's legal background they made a formidable team. By the end of the Seventies, when the FISA v FOCA War threatened the entire fabric of the sport, it was Mosley who thrashed out the Concorde Agreement which became the basis of peace.

In the ultimate poacher-turned-gamekeeper scenario, it was Mosley who challenged dictatorial Frenchman Jean-Marie Balestre for the presidency of FISA, the sport's governing body, in the autumn of 1991. With Ecclestone installed as Vice-President (Promotional Affairs), suddenly they were The Establishment.

A consummate politician, Mosley also became president of the FIA, which has consultative status at both the European Parliament and the United Nations. He steered F1 through a tricky period which followed the death of Ayrton Senna at Imola. He comes across as temperate and softly spoken. But nobody should be fooled. Highly intelligent, he has an inner steel and is as shrewd, articulate and persuasive as any 'real' politician.

As part of the Concorde Agreement settlement negotiated by Mosley in 1980,

> ## 'Highly intelligent, he has an inner steel and is as shrewd, articulate and persuasive as any 'real' politician'

the FIA agreed to lease F1's commercial rights to the teams and FOCA for a four-year period, so long as the teams recognised the governing body's ownership of them. The agreement was always renewed. Increasingly, Ecclestone dealt with commercial matters on his own and took his own financial risks. When Mosley became FIA president and the 1992 Concorde Agreement ran its course, he assigned the commercial rights directly to Ecclestone, cutting out the teams. And it is this contract which forms the basis of Ecclestone's planned stock market flotation. The 1997 season thus ended with dissident teams McLaren, Tyrrell and Williams refusing to sign a new Concorde Agreement unless they were given suitable equity in the new company.

Patrick Head

Patrick Head, 30 percent stakeholder in Williams Grand Prix Engineering, enjoys a reputation as one of the very best and most pragmatic engineers in the F1 paddock. He has been in partnership with Frank Williams for over 20 years and the company prides itself on its low staff turnover under Head's direction.

Born in 1946, he worked at Lola before setting up Williams Grand Prix Engineering with Frank in 1977. His first car was the largely conventional Williams FW06 of 1978. Lotus was making strides with wingcar designs which utilised the underbody airflow to create downforce, but Head says: 'I didn't understand how the Lotus 78 functioned so I steered well clear of it.' Given the performance of FW07 a year later, he learned pretty quickly...

'FW06 was a simple concept,' he adds, 'and it didn't ever see a wind tunnel. I concentrated on clean airflow to the front and rear wings. We didn't have a lot of money but the cars were so simple then. I remember that the engine oil tank was part of the gearbox adaptor, which was reasonably new, especially for a small team. I remember Frank being absolutely apoplectic at the idea. He was desperately worried that it was going to blow up lots of expensive engines.'

Then along came FW07 and Williams had truly arrived. Clay Regazzoni took the team's first victory at Silverstone in 1979 and Alan Jones won more races than World Champion Jody Scheckter.

Head has always advocated simplicity wherever possible but that did not stop him pressing forward with active suspension development as the Eighties became the Nineties. Nigel Mansell had some unhappy experiences with early variants in 1988 but by the winter of 1991 Head was convinced that reliability issues were solved and active was the way forward. He was right. Williams halted McLaren-Honda's four-year domination of F1 with its FW14B in 1992, starting a period of sustained success which lasted until the regulations were changed for 1998 and which was only briefly interrupted by Michael Schumacher's talent in a similarly Renault-powered Benetton in 1995.

With a reputation for engineering excellence under Head, it was both upsetting and unjust that Williams faced criminal charges over Ayrton Senna's fatal accident at Imola in 1994. The Williams record over the past 20 years is first class.

Head is Williams and it is hard to imagine him elsewhere. 'Frank and I have had the occasional spat,' he grins, 'and some challenges would be interesting, but to be effective as a designer you have to have a good facility, good people, enough money and an adequate degree of authority. I've already got that situation and couldn't improve it. There's no point going into a place, deciding how things are going to be, and then finding that all sorts of people are on a different agenda.'

There was one happy story to emerge from Senna's tragically short period at Williams - Head married the Brazilian's former personal assistant, Betisse Assumpcao.

Flavio Briatore

Flavio Briatore was born in Cuneo, near Turin, in 1950. He had a normal Italian childhood and education, studying until he was 18 before starting work as a ski instructor in the Italian Alps. A keen sportsman, he enjoyed the outdoor life for

Clockwise, from bottom left: Professor Sid Watkins; Max Mosley; Tom Walkinshaw; Patrick Head. Flavio Briatore at centre.

a couple of years before moving to Milan to work for the Italian RAS Insurance Company and from there on to the Milan stock exchange.

Briatore met Luciano Benetton in 1974, when the clothing company was in its infancy. He had always been keen on living in America and moved to the USA in 1977, where he worked for the next 12 years running a real estate business and helping to establish Benetton in America.

In 1988 Flavio accompanied Luciano Benetton to Adelaide for the Australian Grand Prix and replaced Peter Collins as team principal the following year.

'I realised that F1 was perfect for communications and for the Benetton Group,' he says, 'but I also knew that it needed to have the right product, which was an attractive and highly competitive team. I appreciated that F1 was the only worldwide sport with such a regular television audience.'

Briatore set about turning Benetton into a winning operation, concentrating on the marketing and commercial side while Tom Walkinshaw was recruited as a shareholder to mastermind engineering.

It was not long before they made their mark. Crucially, they managed to spirit Michael Schumacher away from under Eddie Jordan's nose in some unseemly contract wrangling before the Italian Grand Prix, after Schumacher had made his Grand Prix debut in a Jordan just a fortnight earlier. At the end of the John Barnard era at Benetton, Briatore and Walkinshaw then planned the team's move to a new factory, the Whiteways Technical Centre at Enstone, which gave Benetton one of the best facilities in F1.

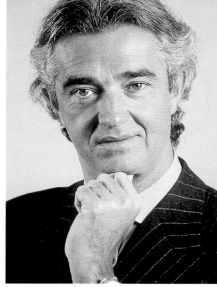

Briatore: Maverick, and missed.

Benetton showed increasing technical competence and Briatore was a colourful part of the F1 scene. He became close friends with Bernie Ecclestone, lived in a sumptuous apartment in Chelsea (bought from Bernie) complete with gold monogrammed FB pillowcases and was never seen without his perma tan.

The 1994 season was traumatic for F1 but Benetton emerged as a major force and Michael Schumacher won the Drivers' World Championship. There was controversy, however, with widespread suspicion that Benetton had used control systems which had been outlawed at the end of 1993. It did not help when Jos Verstappen suffered a refuelling fire at Hockenheim and subsequent inspection of the team's fuel apparatus revealed that a

filter had been illegally removed.

'Hey guys!' Briatore protested when quizzed by the media in Hungary, 'I'm no the technical guy. I don't even know the difference between a fuel filter and a coffee filter. You'd better ask Tom...'

As part of the acrimony over the Benetton situation, Schumacher negotiated a new contract which expired at the end of 1995 instead of '96. He repeated his Drivers' Championship in 1995 and Benetton won its first Constructors' title. Briatore had achieved his ambition. When Schumacher moved on to Ferrari, Benetton suffered a winless 1996 and Briatore's interest seemed to wane. Towards the end of '97 he left the stage to new successor, rallyman David Richards. The tan and the backward baseball cap were gone.

Professor Sid Watkins

'The Prof' is a familiar sight around the Grand Prix circuits of the world. He has been F1's on-track surgeon - not to say guardian - for almost 20 years.

Sid Watkins qualified at Liverpool University Medical School and then trained as a neurosurgeon at the Radcliffe Infirmary, Oxford, where the neurosurgical unit is part of a world renowned head injury and accident service.

Appointed Professor of Neurosurgery in New York in the Sixties, Prof returned to the UK in the Seventies to become the first holder of a similar post at the London Hospital. His research work has contributed to advances in the treatment of Parkinson's disease and cerebral palsy.

Sid's interest in cars dates back to his childhood in Liverpool, where his family

---

The role of the computer

Banks of computer and data acquisition equipment became a prerequisite for Nineties Grand Prix racing. Especially before the technology ban at the end of 1993, the data analyst was king.

Ross Brawn, technical director at Benetton Formula before following Michael Schumacher to Ferrari says: 'It was good fun, but only because we were good at it. It could have been incredibly painful. As a mechanical engineer the problem was that the software engineers were starting to rule, and I guess I wasn't so comfortable about that. Active suspension was getting to the type of level that was beyond my experience or understanding.'

Active suspension allowed precise control of weight distribution and made best use of a tyre's contact patch. It also meant that as a race went on, the car could automatically compensate for such things as changing conditions or varying

fuel loads. And, by keeping the ride height consistent, the car's aerodynamics were optimised.

Active suspension, traction control and four-wheel steering might have been outlawed but computers still play a vital role in F1. Engine ECUs (Electronic Control Units) for example, are capable of two million calculations per second. They control fuel inputs, spark advance and things like over-rev cutouts. Allied to semi-automatic gearboxes, the risk of over-revving an engine on a downchange is now a thing of the past - the computer simply refuses to accept the change if the revs are too high.

With drive-by-wire throttles there is no longer a mechanical link between the throttle and the engine fuelling system. Instead, the throttle opening is controlled by the engine management computer.

Banks of telemetry equipment allow a car to relay information to the pits as it laps the circuit. Engineers can then assess its performance and make alterations. The cars are equipped with sensors which record speed, temperatures, pressures, g-loadings and braking effort. A driver's every move can be scrutinised thoroughly.

Telemetry also allows drivers to dissect their own performance. Laps

can be overlaid on a team-mate's, for example, to compare the effectiveness of various set-ups or simply to see where one driver might be gaining an advantage. Paired with Alain Prost in his first full season at Williams, for example, Damon Hill was able to go away on Friday night, look at Prost's traces and find a substantial amount of time on the second day. At Benetton, meanwhile, Michael Schumacher was protective of his telemetry when Johnny Herbert was his team-mate.

Is it a good thing? Gerhard Berger, for one, once suggested banning telemetry to force more emphasis back on to instinctive feel and increase the role of the driver. But he went unheeded and there are undoubted spin-offs for the motor industry. Never has so much been known by its creators about the workings of an F1 car, and it's all down to computers.

Sid Watkins: guardian angel.

owned a bike shop and garage. While in Oxford he made regular trips to Silverstone and while in the States he regularly worked at Watkins Glen, which led to an invitation to join the RAC medical panel in 1970.

In 1978 he received a phone call from the RAC's Dean Delamont, who told him that a chap by the name of Bernie Ecclestone wanted to speak with him. A meeting was arranged in Sid's office at the London Hospital that night and Ecclestone explained that he wanted Watkins to be responsible for medical care at all Grands Prix. Sid agreed and has since been largely responsible for the great strides made, with the establishment of fully equipped medical centres at each circuit.

When Watkins first took on the position of Grand Prix surgeon in 1978, the first place he travelled to was Sweden, where he was surprised to find that the medical centre was in fact a caravan! He expected Teutonic efficiency at Hockenheim but discovered a converted single decker bus. It had resuscitation and ventilation facilities but there was no anaesthetist and the medical crew camped, slept and cooked alongside the bus, which was parked in the paddock. Things had to change!

Like many medical men, Prof Watkins has an irreverent sense of humour and likes his cigar and glass of red wine or scotch. His presence has become a source of great assurance to more than one generation of drivers and an excellent chase car system has ensured that Sid can be at any accident within seconds of its occurrence. Inevitably he has built up strong friendships with many drivers over the years and came to regard Ayrton Senna as a special friend. Understandably, he sees Imola '94 as the low point of his professional life.

And yet, another one of the old school, insurance specialist Tim Clowes says: 'Sid's an old toughie when it comes to hurting yourself. You've got to be dying. I remember the start of that awful weekend at Imola. I was sitting exactly where Rubens Barrichello had his accident. Sid arrived, looked up at me and said: 'This looks dreadful.' He worked on Rubens, looked up again and said: 'He seems to be all right! Marvellous thing being young isn't it...'

Tom Walkinshaw

Tom Walkinshaw was born in 1946, the son of a Scottish farmer, and was attracted to motorsport by a Mini-racing local garage near his home town of Mauldslie, Lanarkshire.

Walkinshaw started racing Formula Fords in 1968 but it was in saloons that he enjoyed his greatest successes. He won the British Saloon Car Championship in 1980 and '81. He began his link with Jaguar the following year and won the European Touring Car crown in 1984 after six wins which included his second victory in the Spa 24 Hours.

A number of successful associations with major manufacturers led to the establishment of 20 car dealerships (Jaguar, BMW, Rolls Royce, Bentley, Mazda, Volvo and Land Rover). The growth of his business interests and a commission for TWR to run a new Jaguar Sports Prototype programme prompted Walkinshaw to hang up his helmet.

Walkinshaw brought Jaguar three World Championships and two further Le Mans triumphs, and he soon developed links with Holden Special Vehicles in Australia, culminating in success in the Australian Touring Car Championship.

Continued expansion of the TWR Group saw Walkinshaw's company boasting 1500 employees worldwide and a turnover approaching £300 million by the end of 1996.

All that remains to conquer is F1. Walkinshaw acquired a shareholding in Benetton Formula in 1991, where he was engineering director. With Flavio Briatore concentrating on the commercial side, it was Walkinshaw who should take the major credit for Benetton's emergence as a major force in the mid-Nineties. It was Walkinshaw who engineered the signing of Michael Schumacher and the technical progress at the Whiteways Technical Centre at Enstone.

When the FIA found Benetton guilty of a technical irregularity in illegally removing a filter from its refuelling apparatus, at the same time as being in possession of software that made it possible for them to breach the regulations governing control systems, Max Mosley explained that the team had agreed to 'management changes.' At the end of the year Walkinshaw had become engineering director at Ligier, in which Briatore also had an interest.

An inability to gain full control frustrated Walkinshaw and in 1996 TWR entered F1 for the first time in its own right when Walkinshaw bought a controlling interest in Arrows. At a former BT site, he then invested £15m in the new all-purpose Leafield Technical Centre.

Walkinshaw had a reputation as a tough adversary on the track and is as respected throughout the business world. It was typical of him to begin his first year in F1 under his own name with the World Champion in the driving seat. And equally typical for him to be straight talking when he did not approve of Hill's performance level just prior to the British Grand Prix.

The newness of the operation and shortcomings with Yamaha's V10 held Walkinshaw back in year one, but don't expect it to be too long before the team is a major force. Walkinshaw pounced as soon as John Barnard ended his relationship with Ferrari and few would bet against the Scot 'doing a Williams' in the years ahead.

The Top
Five Races

Tony Dodgins

Brilliance in the rain brought Senna his greatest triumph on English soil, Donington 1993.

Donington 1993

Tom Wheatcroft, the owner of Donington Park, had wanted a Grand Prix for a long time. Finally, he got one and Ayrton Senna produced one of those performances that will be talked about for years to come. It was a foul day but Senna's drive warmed anyone there to witness it.

In qualifying the Brazilian had to give best to the dominant Williams-Renaults and to Michael Schumacher's Benetton-Ford. McLaren was a customer Ford team at the time and Senna was still making much of the fact that his HB V8 was not as strong as the 'works' engines in the Benetton.

On race day it mattered little. Senna did not make the best of starts and he was beaten into the first corner and forced wide by Schumacher's Benetton, which also allowed Wendlinger's Sauber past the pair of them. Undeterred, Senna stepped around the Benetton at Redgate and then sliced past Wendlinger on the outside of the Craner Curves. Hill was despatched at McLeans and then Prost was outbraked for the lead at the Melbourne Hairpin.

Senna was in a league of his own, although Prost's race was compromised by an unfortunate calling of the wet-dry conditions which resulted in no fewer than seven pit stops. Senna called five times but took on fresh rubber on only four of his visits. On lap 57 he drove straight through the pits and recorded the race's fastest lap!

Hill was almost a minute and a half behind in second place when the chequered flag fell. The day was also memorable for Rubens Barrichello's fine drive in his third race for Jordan. He ran a solid third, ahead of Prost, until cruelly running short of fuel six laps from the end.

Adelaide 1993

It was circumstance as much as anything. It had been intense rivalry. At times, even deep-seated hatred. The seeds lay in those two years which Ayrton Senna and Alain Prost spent together at McLaren in 1988-'89. And then there was the second of their championship deciding incidents at Suzuka when Prost had moved on to Ferrari.

This was it. Prost had won his fourth world title with Williams in 1993 but Frank had signed Senna for '94. Alain had opted for retirement and, after 51 wins and 198 starts, was lining up for his last race.

Senna, meanwhile, was having his last Grand Prix for Ron Dennis after six years and three World Championships with McLaren. Before the race, Prost said there would be no rapprochement between the two. He had offered his hand before and Senna had turned him down. So why now, just because he was retiring?

There had been bad blood between them at Silverstone where Senna's defence of an early second place was generally adjudged to be far too intimidatory. Now it was their last head-to-head and both men were determined to win.

For Senna, as ever, the intensity ran deeper. He had been unable to compete with Prost's superior Williams FW15 for much of the year but McLaren had made strides with the MP4/8 towards the end of the season and Senna had won impressively at Suzuka. On the steets of Adelaide he thought he could do so again. He took the pole with Alain alongside on the front row. Senna was emotional before the start whenever friends such as Jo Ramirez came close. Keeping the lid on his feelings, he made the better start, drove with total commitment and at flag fall was nine seconds clear of the Williams. On the podium, Prost, sensing the poignancy of the moment, raised his bitter rival's arm aloft.

Senna had scored McLaren's 104th victory, eclipsing Ferrari, and there was a long embrace from Ron Dennis. Tina Turner, in Adelaide for the season-closing concert, hauled Senna on stage for Simply the Best. It wasn't just the end of the season but the end of an era. Everybody felt it. What we didn't know at the time, it was to be Ayrton's final victory... ➡

End of the road for Schumacher at Jerez in 1997 (far left). Below, Senna celebrates his final victory, Adelaide 1993.

At a time when Grand Prix racing was intent on improving safety by slowing down cars, and with chicane blight emasculating circuits, the re-introduction of refuelling flew in the face of logic.

The concept was banned in the early Eighties but it was back for 1994 as a means of spicing up the show and making for better television. Whether it was successful or not was another matter. It seemed to break up as many battles as it created.

It is worth recalling the circumstances of its reintroduction. During a crisis meeting at Hockenheim in 1993, in which leading teams were anxious to delay the active suspension ban as long as possible, Bernie Eccletone threw in refuelling at the end of proceedings, almost as an afterthought. Everybody agreed to it but a few weeks later there had been a rethink. Ecclestone himself didn't seem too bothered either way, but unanimous agreement was needed for a reversal and Ferrari was in favour of refuelling. The Scuderia, it should be remembered, was the only one to use a thirst V12 engine...

Many predicted a conflagration in the pits and there was concern over liability insurance among other things. At Hockenheim in 1994 it happened, and Jos Verstappen and seven Benetton team members were fortunate to escape serious injury, though several of them needed hospital treatment.

'I have always been against it,' Ron Dennis stated. 'Danger is part of motor racing but refuelling is an artificial danger added by the sport's governing body.' Frank Williams agreed: 'I am totally against it because of the human element.'

Benetton boss Flavio Briatore called for an immediate ban on refuelling in the aftermath of his team's accident, but the sentiment did not enjoy anything like unanimous support.

Ferrari sporting director Jean Todt pointed out that all teams had given unanimous consent for its return and a number of people thought that if it was an integral part of both IndyCar and sportscar racing, then F1, as the pinnacle of motorsport, should be able to accommodate it without too much problem.

Eddie Irvine later suffered a scare when Jordan had a refuelling incident at Spa in 1995 and Pacific had a lucky escape too, although a crew member sustained a serious knee injury as Andrea Montermini's car left with the hose still attached. Pedro Diniz's Ligier was also consumed by fire in Argentina in 1996, after a fuel system malfunction.

Recently, refuelling stops have been incident free and refinements were made to the Intertechnique refuelling apparatus, but many are still concerned that it is an accident waiting to happen.

The appalling conditions are obvious as the 1994 Japanese GP gets underway at Suzuka.

Suzuka 1994

The 1994 season embraced tragedy and controversy. Damon Hill, thrust uneasily into the role of Williams team leader by Ayrton Senna's accident at Imola, responded magnificently. His confidence soared when he saw off the challenge of Nigel Mansell, who made a guest appearance for Williams at Magny-Cours.

Michael Schumacher had been runaway championship leader before being disqualified from second place at Silverstone, losing his win at Spa and suffering a two-race ban. Hill had turned it into a contest by winning at Monza and Estoril in Schumacher's absence.

Schumacher returned at Jerez and scored a decisive win to give himself a four-point margin over Hill with Suzuka and Adelaide remaining.

Schumacher's Benetton took pole ahead of Hill in Japan, where appalling wet conditions confronted drivers at the start.

Hill celebrates a brilliant win.

> ## 'His confidence soared when he saw off the challenge of Nigel Mansell...'

Schumacher led away and opened out an 8.6s advantage after the Safety Car had appeared due to cars going off on the straight! The race was red-flagged when Martin Brundle aquaplaned off the road and injured a marshal. At the restart Schumacher made an early stop and was then held up behind Mika Hakkinen's McLaren. Hill enjoyed a 7.5s advantage after his stop seven laps later, but Schumacher ate into it and retook an aggregate lead on lap 35. Benetton, however, had gambled on the race being called at 75 percent distance, the earliest opportunity at which it would qualify for full points. But conditions improved and it ran its course, necessitating an extra fuel stop for Schumacher.

With 10 laps to go, he charged back into the race 14.5s adrift of Hill. They were not together on the road but the aggregate gap was all-important. Schumacher was charging and Hill's task was not helped by the right rear jamming on during his only pit stop. He'd only been able to take on three fresh tyres.

Schumacher closed in relentlessly but Hill was equal to the challenge and finished 3.6s ahead on aggregate time. It had been a superb display by both men, with lap times in the mid 1m 56s bracket as against the race's next quickest lap, from Nigel Mansell, at 1m 57.9s. It took the championship down to the wire in Adelaide and we know what happened there!

Monaco 1996

Okay, so Damon Hill and Jean Alesi retired and Michael Schumacher helped by hitting the wall, but if anyone deserved an appointment with Prince Rainier at Monte Carlo in 1996 it was Olivier Panis.

Panis started 14th after a throttle problem spoiled his qualifying. Sunday, he knew, was likely to be frustrating. He was quickest in the race morning warm-up but from the second half of the grid it promised to be a long afternoon.

Olivier completed a wet opening lap in 12th place, the first 2.06 miles taking the Ligier 2m 11.6s while Damon Hill's lap at the front cost the Williams just 1m 56.03s. 'I noticed that Brundle was having problems under acceleration and I got past him out of the Rascasse complex,' Panis explained. So, with seven laps down, he was 11th, but already a massive 40s behind Hill. Berger's disappearance put him into the top 10.

Now Panis was behind Mika Hakkinen. The McLaren was despatched on the run down from Casino Square into Mirabeau. Ninth. Further up the road, Frentzen lost patience behind Irvine's Ferrari and removed his front wing, requiring an extra visit to the pits. Eighth.

Irvine's Ferrari ran third with Coulthard's McLaren, Villeneuve's Williams, Salo's Tyrrell and Herbert's Sauber all breathing down its neck. It was a typical Monaco train and Panis calmly tacked on to the end. He soon sliced inside Herbert into the Loews Hairpin. Seventh.

An early stop for slicks as the track dried leapfrogged the Ligier up to fourth. Panis took 18s out of Hill's lead over the next 10 laps! Such pace brought him on to Irvine's tail and another do or die move at the Loews Hairpin put Olivier third. He had now passed Brundle, Hakkinen, Herbert and Irvine in full racing situations around the reputedly impossible confines of Monaco. Phenomenal in itself.

When Hill blew up and

He came, he saw and, to everyone's surprise, he conquered. Olivier Panis (above, and below with David Coulthard and Johnny Herbert on the podium) was in stunning form at Monaco in 1996.

Alesi's Benetton broke a spring, Panis led! He had to repel a late challenge from Coulthard, who was driving in a helmet borrowed from Schumacher, and all the while the Ligier crew was worried about whether he had enough fuel to make it to the end. He did. Just. It was a superb drive and a deserved win.

Jerez 1997

It had everything. A head-to-head between Jacques Villeneuve and Michael Schumacher for the world title and the possibility of Ferrari's first Drivers' Championship since Jody Scheckter 18 years earlier.

Schumacher came into the race with a single point advantage over his Williams adversary. At Adelaide three years earlier he had enjoyed the same margin over Hill going into the final race. And observers were not slow to recall what happened then. Schumacher, though, vowed to do it cleanly.

You knew this was going to be no ordinary race when the top three all qualified on exactly 1m 21.072s! And the first two were the championship protagonists! Villeneuve took pole by dint of having recorded the time first, Schumacher started alongside him and Villeneuve's Williams team-mate Heinz-Harald Frentzen was third.

Schumacher's Ferrari made the best start and opened up an early margin over Frentzen, who couldn't run quickly enough. Heinz-Harald moved over for Villeneuve, who started to trade fastest laps with Schumacher. The pair were flat-out.

Schumacher stopped first and Williams dropped Frentzen back into the Ferrari's pit stop window to slow it down. This was successfully accomplished so that Villeneuve could make his stop and ease on to Schumacher's tail. Schumacher had lost a five-second advantage but got half of it back when Norberto Fontana in the Sauber - which used Ferrari engines - let him by but then held up Villeneuve for the best part of a lap.

Villeneuve gradually clawed back some of the deficit and as the pair made their final stops there was two seconds between them. Schumacher found his car over a second slower on his final set of tyres and Villeneuve caught him napping with a late dive up the inside at Dry Sack on lap 48. Schumacher panicked and cynically turned in to the Williams' sidepod. This time he came off worse. The Ferrari bounced off into the gravel trap and Villeneuve was able to stroke to the championship, moving over for the McLarens of Hakkinen and Coulthard on the final lap. The incident cost Schumacher many admirers but, after an FIA disciplinary hearing, precious little else.

'The Ferrari revival' became one of the most overworked cliches of the 1997 season but Niki Lauda, who took much of the credit for turning Ferrari around in the mid-Seventies, insists it was a reality despite the fact that Michael Schumacher missed out on the championship at the last round.

Lauda sees a parallel with the Seventies. 'I think Ross Brawn made a big difference and the team performed very well, no question.'

Brawn himself thinks that in the days of working with John Barnard's Guildford-based FDD, the Italian side of the Ferrari operation lacked a technical reference point. 'People needed to know what they should be doing and it's difficult to do that over a phone,' he asserts. 'Giorgio Ascanelli was doing a good job on the racing side but it was needed for design and manufacture as well. Barnard was a bit too remote and I don't think he'd deny that.'

Ferrari chief mechanic Nigel Stepney puts the improvement down to basics. 'It was largely because we didn't change the whole car or play with major things like the gearbox. We had a good programme at the beginning of the season, the car was on time from FDD and we had a solid

base. We did a lot of testing early on, which we've never managed since I've been at Ferrari. It was always planned, but to achieve it was hard for us. Now we can do it. We have the people, the organisation and we are able to programme correctly. The car wasn't dramatically different from what we'd had before. It was a progression and that's what everybody else does.

'The whole team, engineering-wise, worked extremely efficiently. When Ross Brawn first saw how young the guys were he couldn't believe it, but he soon admitted that the level was good. We have a good squad and it's a calmer than usual group of people. They work well under pressure. And they are *allowed* to work under pressure. Before, without Jean Todt, it was very hard to work. Now he takes all the flak. Before there was a lot of internal pressure and the whole thing was very disorganised. He's allowed to work like a normal team. Williams had the better car, but we had the better team.'

Schumacher's race engineer, Ignazio Lunetta, adds: 'A big difference this year was the atmosphere in the team. There was less panic and more thoughtful action rather than instinctive reaction. But we were basically the same people with a year's more experience and better organisation.

'The car was easier to work on as well. Everything was positioned correctly and you could change the mechanical or aerodynamic set-up without a long job.'

Ferrari worked hard to overcome the basic fact that its F310B was no Williams FW19 despite being a lot better than anyone gave it credit for. A revised chassis mid-season was necessary to allow a bigger fuel tank for the thirstier second evolution 046 V10 engine, but Ferrari also took the opportunity to pare some weight.

Since his recruitment to the Ferrari fold in 1993, Todt had assembled key people in key technical areas. Many of them, like Brawn, designer Rory Byrne, aerodynamicist Willem Toet and electronics experts Tad Czapski were ex-Benetton, from the Schumacher era. But with the world's best driver undoubtedly on the McLaren-Mercedes shopping list, will 1998 be the last chance to complete the revival proper?

F1: non-contact sport or a boxing match?

David Tremayne

When Ayrton Senna drove into the back end of Alain Prost's Ferrari in the first corner of the Japanese Grand Prix at Suzuka in 1990, F1 changed irrevocably.

There had been incidents in the past, inevitably, when drivers had clashed on the circuit. Stewart and Regazzoni at the Nurburgring in 1972; Fittipaldi and Scheckter at Paul Ricard in 1973; Senna had felt the grip of Mansell's fingers after a tangle at Spa in 1987; and Senna had weaved at Prost at Estoril in 1988. A year later they had bumped at Suzuka when Prost blocked Senna going into the chicane. Most of the time they were genuine racing incidents, the inevitable corollary of two men fighting for the same piece of road.

But the 1990 Suzuka Incident was something very different. For the first time one driver deliberately drove his car into another's with the specific intent of taking him out of the race. Witnesses confirmed that the engine note of Senna's McLaren-Honda never varied as he kept his foot hard on the throttle even as Prost turned into the corner inches ahead of him. McLaren representatives, who had worked with Prost in the past, privately consoled him and apologised.

A year later Senna admitted everything. As he was celebrating the victory in Suzuka that he had just gifted to team-mate Gerhard Berger, and the second place which had confirmed his third and final World Championship, he suddenly let himself be provoked into an extraordinary outburst. He confessed that it all went back to 1989, when he had clashed with Prost and then been denied a glowing victory. He had deliberately taken Prost off, 'because I decided that if he got into the corner ahead of me, he wasn't gonna make it round.'

No action was taken against Ayrton Senna that bleak day, October 21 1990, nor one year later on.

The old-timers, men who respected the traditions of the sport and the honour of others they had raced wheel-to-wheel, were outraged.

'You get things that seem like invitations to try and pass all the time,' Jackie Stewart said. 'The thing is to decide which ones to accept and which to reject.' In Adelaide in 1990 he had a public spat with Senna when he asked him, for Australian television, why he had by then had 21 incidents with other drivers.

'You always see gaps in racing,' said Mario Andretti, who would be the first to admit that he himself could be a little impetuous (but never, ever dirty). 'The trick is to make sure they're wider than your car...'

Even Senna's most ardent fans were appalled during the opening laps of the British GP at Silverstone in 1993 when he weaved and darted all over the track in a wild attempt to keep Prost's markedly quicker Williams at bay. Such tactics simply were not acceptable. Yet they had now become a part of racing, thanks to the inactivity of the governing body.

In the Brazilian GP earlier that year Michael Schumacher finished third, then grabbed everyone's attention by launching into a stinging attack on Senna's driving at the post-race press conference. But as events were to show, that was the pot calling the kettle black.

In 1994 Schumacher and Hill went to the Australian GP in Adelaide one point apart, for the World Championship finale. Schumacher hit a wall, and as Hill tried to take advantage of the damaged Benetton, Schumacher deliberately turned into him.

Ayrton Senna, the flawed genius whose bullying tactics gave birth to a whole new code of driving conduct.

The rise and rise of Williams

By the end of the 1997 Grand Prix season, special congratulations were due to Williams Grand Prix Engineering. Frank's men had won a record ninth Constructors' Championship, a phenomenal achievement considering that the team was founded just 20 years previously and did not win its first Grand Prix until 1979, when Clay Regazzoni was first across the line at Silverstone.

Williams started the year with the best win-to-start ratio in F1 and improved it still further, to 103 out of 379 for a 27.17 percent success rate. Its next target has to be the greatest overall number of race wins. Two teams sat ahead of it at the end of the 1997 season - McLaren on 107 and Ferrari on 113.

If McLaren dominated the mid-Eighties and early Nineties, Williams took its early Eighties control back with the superb active FW14B which took Nigel Mansell to the World Championship in 1992. Technical director Patrick Head was the first to acknowledge that much of the credit belonged to Adrian Newey, who joined Williams as chief designer from the Leyton House March team.

The theme continued in 1993 when Alain Prost took over where Mansell left off and won his fourth world title after a sabbatical year when he was fired by Ferrari in 1991. Prost then announced his retirement when he got wind that Ayrton Senna was coming to Williams for 1994. That season was the most traumatic in the team's history with Senna's fatal accident at Imola. The FW16 proved difficult at first but was the class of the field by the year end. The team proved its character and mettle when Damon Hill grew superbly into the role of team leader and Williams emerged with another Constructors' title.

Bested by Schumacher's brilliance at Benetton in 1995, Williams hit back with Drivers'/Constructors' Championship doubles in 1996/'97. But when Newey was poached by McLaren and began work at Woking on August 1 1997, questions were asked about Williams' ability to sustain its position of dominance. Especially with the additional loss of engine manufacturer at the end of 1997.

The Williams team is bigger than Newey or any one individual, but F1 goes in cycles and it would be astonishing if Williams can sustain the level of dominance it has shown in the Nineties while undergoing changes of technical partner - BMW becomes the team's engine supplier for the year 2000. But who knows? It is a team that nobody underestimates.

Rough and tumble. Schumacher chops Hill in Adelaide 1994 (above), while Senna bullies Prost, Silverstone 1993 (below).

Both retired, and Schumacher won his first World Championship.

By contrast, Hill's unsuccessful efforts to pass Schumacher at Silverstone and Monza in 1995 were far from deliberate attacks; they were merely ill-judged and ill-executed and resulted in both men going off the road. Later, after Schumacher had carved him up royally in a dice at Spa, when Damon was on wet tyres and Michael slicks at the wettest point of the Belgian GP, Hill called upon the FIA to clarify precisely what constituted acceptable tactics.

In the past things had tended to be self-regulating. Of the Sixties, Dan Gurney once said: 'Wild guys tended to weed themselves out in a hurry. You just hoped they didn't take one of the good guys with them.' But now Hill was branded a wimp by the popular media. Like his father Graham, he had a strong sense of right and wrong and no intention of gutter brawling. But that, it seemed, was what an increasingly lay television audience wanted, as if F1 had suddenly become a cross between banger racing and wrestling.

'I think Michael is prepared to do anything necessary to win, including not letting the other person past,' Hill said. 'He's a hard customer. It's really a matter of pursuing your own line of ethics, where you draw that line and what tactics you employ.

'I think motor racing is very much like boxing. You end up with two people out there, focusing on trying to beat each other. It's usually your team-mate; that's the normal situation because your team-mate is always the first man you've got to beat. But whoever it is, you do tend to find that the competitive urge makes it necessary to feel some sort of degree of aggression to the other person. But the idea is to control that and to channel it positively, to make yourself perform better. That's what sport is for, isn't it? It's an alternative for aggression.

'Some people suggest that these days sport should be like a public boxing match, pushing and shoving and no regard for the rules, but I don't care for that. I could weave all over the track, I could knock the other guy off. But it's not in the rules. The rules are that you don't do it. If I did it I'd get a ban.

'People suggest that all this weaving Michael has been doing is the sort of thing that could happen when you go and watch kids racing karts. Well, you know what happens then? They go over the top of each other and break each other's necks... That's what happens.'

He was asked whether Schumacher is in the same mould as Ayrton Senna, having raced wheel-to-wheel with both, but replied: 'It's not for me to say. Ayrton wasn't a saint, was he? He was in the business to win, and he was pretty ruthless when it came to that. I mean, I don't agree with driving into the back of someone at the start of the race, just to make sure that they don't have the chance of winning the championship. I didn't agree with it at half past three in the morning when I got up to watch the Japanese Grand Prix on television in 1990. I was really irritated. We missed out on a good race.

'Alternatively, when Alain was racing there at Suzuka the previous year, he did

what he was entitled to do, which was to turn into the corner. It wasn't as if Ayrton had not pushed him to the very limit of what he could endure, with that particular brand of intimidation that he used. At that point what Alain did was perfectly within the rules.

'But it is the spirit of the thing that has suffered. The times have changed and the ethics have changed. You just have to make your own choice, don't you? And then live with it. Michael obviously has, and so have I.'

> ## 'That's what sport is for, isn't it? It's an alternative for aggression.'

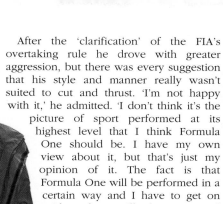

After the 'clarification' of the FIA's overtaking rule he drove with greater aggression, but there was every suggestion that his style and manner really wasn't suited to cut and thrust. 'I'm not happy with it,' he admitted. 'I don't think it's the picture of sport performed at its highest level that I think Formula One should be. I have my own view about it, but that's just my opinion of it. The fact is that Formula One will be performed in a certain way and I have to get on with what will be accepted practise. I can't change it to suit me.'

Schumacher's deliberate swerve into Jacques Villeneuve at Jerez, during the GP of Europe which decided the 1997 title, brought an era to an end which became even more controversial when an FIA World Motor Sport Council meeting refused to ban him. 'It came to the conclusion that although Michael Schumacher acted deliberately,' said FIA president Max Mosley, drawing a semantic distinction, 'it was instinctive and not premeditated. Careful consideration was given to banning him for 1998 but it concluded that to do so would be futile, because there is no driver competing in 1998 who would not be ready to accept a ban in 1999 if he could win the championship in 1998. So it would not be a deterrent in any sense.'

As Prost turns in, Senna refuses to lift off. Suzuka 1990.

A passionate guardian of the sport's ethics and morals, an exasperated Stewart said: 'Guys like Jim Clark, Graham Hill, Dan Gurney and Denny Hulme would never have done what Michael did. Neither would Stirling Moss or Fangio. Every young driver will have seen that, and if they see someone getting away with it that behaviour will then be mirrored in every other form of motorsport. If something isn't done, eventually there is going to be a massive accident.'

Meanwhile, Schumacher had his second place in the World Championship annulled and was required to do 'community service' assisting the FIA with, of all things, a road safety campaign.

'I think,' Stewart said at Gleneagles not long afterwards, 'that we need to get more sport back into F1.' But his seemed a lone, though mercifully strident, voice as the World Championship moved beyond its half century.

Michael Schumacher (above with 1997 Nemesis Jacques Villeneuve) is Senna's heir apparent, but also inherited his on-track ruthlessness.

F1.50 Statistics

World Champions

1950	Giuseppe Farina (Italy)	1974	Emerson Fittipaldi (Brazil)
1951	Juan Manuel Fangio (Argentina)	1975	Niki Lauda (Austria)
1952	Alberto Ascari (Italy)	1976	James Hunt (Britain)
1953	Alberto Ascari (Italy)	1977	Niki Lauda (Austria)
1954	Juan Manuel Fangio (Argentina)	1978	Mario Andretti (America)
1955	Juan Manuel Fangio (Argentina)	1979	Jody Scheckter (South Africa)
1956	Juan Manuel Fangio (Argentina)	1980	Alan Jones (Australia)
1957	Juan Manuel Fangio (Argentina)	1981	Nelson Piquet (Brazil)
1958	Mike Hawthorn (Britain)	1982	Keke Rosberg (Finland)
1959	Jack Brabham (Australia)	1983	Nelson Piquet (Brazil)
1960	Jack Brabham (Australia)	1984	Niki Lauda (Austria)
1961	Phil Hill (America)	1985	Alain Prost (France)
1962	Graham Hill (Britain)	1986	Alain Prost (France)
1963	Jim Clark (Britain)	1987	Nelson Piquet (Brazil)
1964	John Surtees (Britain)	1988	Ayrton Senna (Brazil)
1965	Jim Clark (Britain)	1989	Alain Prost (France)
1966	Jack Brabham (Australia)	1990	Ayrton Senna (Brazil)
1967	Denny Hulme (New Zealand)	1991	Ayrton Senna (Brazil)
1968	Graham Hill (Britain)	1992	Nigel Mansell (Britain)
1969	Jackie Stewart (Britain)	1993	Alain Prost (France)
1970	Jochen Rindt (Austria)	1994	Michael Schumacher (Germany)
1971	Jackie Stewart (Britain)	1995	Michael Schumacher (Germany)
1972	Emerson Fittipaldi (Brazil)	1996	Damon Hill (Britain)
1973	Jackie Stewart (Britain)	1997	Jacques Villeneuve (Canada)

World Champion Constructors

Year	Constructor	Year	Constructor
1958	Vanwall (Britain)	1978	Lotus (Britain)
1959	Cooper (Britain)	1979	Ferrari (Italy)
1960	Cooper (Britain)	1980	Williams (Britain)
1961	Ferrari (Italy)	1981	Williams (Britain)
1962	BRM (Britain)	1982	Ferrari (Italy)
1963	Lotus (Britain)	1983	Ferrari (Italy)
1964	Ferrari (Italy)	1984	McLaren (Britain)
1965	Lotus (Britain)	1985	McLaren (Britain)
1966	Brabham (Britain)	1986	Williams (Britain)
1967	Brabham (Britain)	1987	Williams (Britain)
1968	Lotus (Britain)	1988	McLaren (Britain)
1969	Matra (France)	1989	McLaren (Britain)
1970	Lotus (Britain)	1990	McLaren (Britain)
1971	Tyrrell (Britain)	1991	McLaren (Britain)
1972	Lotus (Britain)	1992	Williams (Britain)
1973	Lotus (Britain)	1993	Williams (Britain)
1974	McLaren (Britain)	1994	Williams (Britain)
1975	Ferrari (Italy)	1995	Benetton (Britain)
1976	Ferrari (Italy)	1996	Williams (Britain)
1977	Ferrari (Italy)	1997	Williams (Britain)

Greatest number of wins - *drivers*

1	Alain Prost 51
2	Ayrton Senna 41
3	Nigel Mansell 31
4	Jackie Stewart 27
	Michael Schumacher 27
6	Jim Clark 25
	Niki Lauda 25
8	Juan Manuel Fangio 24
9	Nelson Piquet 23
10	Damon Hill 21

Greatest number of wins - *teams*

1	Ferrari 113
2	McLaren 107
3	Williams 103
4	Lotus 79
5	Brabham 35
6	Benetton 27
7	Tyrrell 23
8	BRM 17
9	Cooper 16
10	Renault (France) 15

Greatest number of wins per season - *drivers*

1	Nigel Mansell 9 - 1992
	Michael Schumacher 9 - 1995
3	Ayrton Senna 8 - 1988
	Michael Schumacher 8 - 1994
	Damon Hill 8 - 1996
6	Jim Clark 7 - 1963
	Alain Prost 7 - 1984, '88, '93
	Ayrton Senna 7 - 1991
	Jacques Villeneuve 7 - 1997
10	Alberto Ascari 6 - 1952
	Juan Manuel Fangio 6 - 1954
	Jim Clark 6 - 1965
	James Hunt 6 - 1976
	Mario Andretti 6 - 1978
	Nigel Mansell 6 - 1987
	Ayrton Senna 6 - 1989, '90
	Damon Hill 6 - 1994

Greatest number of wins per season - *teams*

1	McLaren 15 - 1988
2	McLaren 12 - 1984
	Williams 12 - 1996
4	Benetton 11 - 1995
5	McLaren 10 - 1989
	Williams 10 - 1992, '93
7	Williams 9 - 1986, '87
8	Lotus 8 - 1978
	McLaren 8 - 1991
	Benetton 8 - 1994
	Williams 8 - 1997

The World Champions' engines

1	Ford (Britain) 13 - 1968; '69; '70; '71; '72; '73; '74; '76; '78; '80; '81; '82; '94
2	Ferrari (Italy) 9 - 1952; '53; '56; '58; '61; '64; '75; '77; '79
3	Honda (Japan) 5 - 1987; '88; '89; '90; '91
	Renault (France) 5 1992; '93; '95; '96; '97
5	Coventry Climax (Britain) 4 - 1959; '60; '63; '65
6	Porsche (Germany) 3 - 1984; '85; '86
7	Alfa Romeo (Italy) 2 - 1950; '51
	Mercedes (Germany) 2 - 1954; '55
	Maserati (Italy) 2 - 1954; '57
	Repco (Australia) 2 1966; '67

Greatest number of pole positions - *drivers*

1	Ayrton Senna 65
2	Jim Clark 33
	Alain Prost 33
4	Nigel Mansell 32
5	Juan Manuel Fangio 28
6	Niki Lauda 24
	Nelson Piquet 24
8	Damon Hill 20
9	Mario Andretti 18
10	Jackie Stewart 17
	Michael Schumacher 17

Greatest number of pole positions - *teams*

1	Ferrari 121
2	Williams 108
3	Lotus 107
4	McLaren 80
5	Brabham 39
6	Renault 31
7	Benetton 15
8	Tyrrell 14
9	Alfa Romeo 12
10	BRM 11

Greatest number of fastest laps
- drivers

1	Alain Prost 41
2	Nigel Mansell 30
3	Jim Clark 28
	Michael Schumacher 28
5	Niki Lauda 25
6	Juan Manuel Fangio 23
	Nelson Piquet 23
8	Gerhard Berger (Austria) 21
9	Stirling Moss (Britain) 20
10	Ayrton Senna 19
	Damon Hill 19

Greatest number of Grand Prix participations
- drivers

1	Riccardo Patrese (Italy) 256
2	Gerhard Berger (Austria) 210
3	Andrea de Cesaris (Italy) 208
4	Nelson Piquet (Brazil) 204
5	Alain Prost (France) 199
6	Michele Alboreto (Italy) 194
7	Nigel Mansell (Britain) 187
8	Graham Hill (Britain) 176
9	Jacques Laffite (France) 175
10	Niki Lauda (Austria) 171

Greatest number of fastest laps
- teams

1	Ferrari 127
2	Williams 109
3	Lotus 71
	McLaren 71
5	Brabham 40
6	Benetton 34
7	Tyrrell 20
8	Renault 18
9	Maserati 15
	BRM 15

Greatest number of Grand Prix participations
- teams

1	Ferrari 587
2	Lotus 490
3	McLaren 460
4	Brabham 399
5	Tyrrell 402
6	Williams 379
7	Prost (formerly Ligier) (France) 343
8	Arrows (Britain) 305
9	Benetton 251
10	March (Britain) 231

Team Profiles

Mark Hughes

Ferrari

F1 entry:	**1950**
Races/Victories:	**587/113**
Drivers' Championships:	**9**
Constructors' Championships:	**8**
Pole positions:	**121**
Fastest laps:	**127**

After years of falling increasingly behind during F1's most technologically intense era, Ferrari is finally making up lost ground and going some way towards living up to its legend. Sure, much of it is the 'Schumacher effect' which so transformed Benetton, but a team at least needs to be in the ballpark to make any worthwhile use of a talent like his, and for much of the recent past Ferrari hasn't even fallen into that category. That it does today is thanks to an unusually enduring regime headed by Luca di Montezemolo, who masterminded the team's success in the mid-Seventies and returned as president in 1992.

Ferrari has won its drivers eight World Championships but the last of these was in 1979. Between then and the new Montezemolo era, a discontinuous technical regime and political recriminations at failure tended to hamstring real progress.

When Montezemolo returned in 1992 Ferrari was in a real mess; Alain Prost had been sacked for daring to be critical in public, and technically the team had fallen far behind the standards being set by Williams and McLaren. The F92A proved to be overcomplicated, ineffective and unreliable.

The path between that sorry state and the team which went head-to-head with Williams for the 1997 World Championship has not been a straightforward one. But among a myriad of changes there have been three critical elements. The first of these was to get the engine department to forget tradition and replace its powerful but thirsty V12s with more efficient V10s. The second was to hire former Peugeot team manager Jean Todt in a similar position at Ferrari. He joined in mid-1993, bringing with him a formidable reputation for organisational efficiency.

The third was the hiring of Michael Schumacher for 1996. Bringing the world's best driver on board in the dark days of 1992 would have been a waste of money. That it was not so now was down to the changes instigated by Montezemolo and implemented by Todt. The 1996 Ferrari F310 was not the best car in the field, but it was good enough to give Schumacher three victories.

He brought more than just driving ability with him. He joined on his own terms, with his own agenda and his own ideas of how best to follow it through. An old-style Ferrari organisation - the sort of team it was in 1991 when it sacked Prost - would have had big problems accommodating such a man. The Montezemolo-era Ferrari recognised what it was gaining and has allowed Schumacher to mould the team around him, hence the presence of the former Benetton technical men Ross Brawn and Rory Byrne.

These three - Schumacher, Brawn and Byrne - guided tactically by Todt and strategically by Montezemolo formed the core of the team which almost won the world title in 1997 and is perhaps the hottest favourite to do so in 1998.

For almost one hundred years,

Castrol has been helping drivers

get from point A to point B.

Jacques Villeneuve -1997 F1 World Drivers' Champion
Rothmans Williams Renault -1997 F1 Constructors Champion

Some faster than others.

It's an honour to be entering the 50th anniversary of F1 as part of the reigning world champion Williams Team.
But then that's why we're revved up and ready to race – as long as there's a point B in sight.

DRIVE HARD

McLaren

F1 entry:	**1966**
Races/Victories:	**460/106**
Drivers' Championships:	**9**
Constructors' Championships:	**7**
Pole positions:	**80**
Fastest laps:	**71**

The former superteam which took all before it - it won all but one Grand Prix in 1988 - has been going through a phase of regrouping ever since it lost, successively, its dominant Honda engines and Ayrton Senna. The signs in 1997 were that the corner had finally been turned and that McLaren was on the way back.

The team that Bruce McLaren set up in the mid-Sixties would be unrecognisable were he around to see it today. That team, in essence, stayed together until part-way through 1980 when it merged with an F2 team, Project 4, headed by former Cooper and Brabham mechanic Ron Dennis. This was the birth of McLaren International, which has vied with Williams Grand Prix Engineering as the most successful F1 team of modern times. Within a year of the merger, none of the key personnel from the old McLaren remained.

With John Barnard's pioneering carbon-fibre cars, the new-era McLaren took consecutive world titles in 1984, '85 and '86. But in 1987 McLaren won just three races - a barren season by its standards and prospects looked even more worrying when Barnard had a fundamental disagreement with Dennis and left.

Dennis' retort was formidable. He managed to negotiate a Honda engine deal to replace his ageing Porsche motors, at the expense of Williams which had just delivered Honda a World Championship! The Honda link then massaged into place the driver that Dennis had for some time being trying to pair with Prost, Ayrton Senna. With the possible exception of Tazio Nuvolari and Achille Varzi in the Thirties or Juan Manuel Fangio and Stirling Moss in the Fifties this was perhaps the strongest driver pairing there has ever been.

Between them, as the best drivers in the best cars, run by the best team, Senna and Prost won 15 of 1988's 16 Grands Prix, Senna taking eight and the title. It was the sort of dominance previously thought impossible in the modern era of F1 and stands as testimony to the vision and tenacity of Dennis.

Further titles followed in 1989, '90 and '91 but there were murmurs that the success was down to a combination of Honda horsepower, the genius of the McLaren drivers and the continuing greatness of McLaren as a team. The chassis, it was suggested, were not as good as the Barnard Ferrari's or that of the Williams.

Honda's retirement at the end of 1992 and Senna's defection to Williams a year later were critical blows. Mika Hakkinen, fast and spectacular but without the all-round greatness of Senna, took over as de facto number one driver and an engine partner was found in Peugeot, new to F1 but keen to take on marketplace rival Renault. It wasn't a great relationship and when the opportunity of a partnership with Mercedes came along, Peugeot was dropped like a stone.

From 1995 to '97 the Mercedes motors have made constant progress to the point where they are probably the best part of the car. McLaren is almost back to where it was in the last days of its Honda partnership - only without a Senna or a Schumacher. David Coulthard gave the team a couple of breakthrough wins in 1997, Hakkinen a more dubious one at the season finale, and the team is still strategically perhaps the best in the business. But what is really needed now is a chassis to match that of a Williams. The chances are, that's exactly what it will have in 1998 when the wraps come off the first McLaren to be penned by former Williams aerodynamicist Adrian Newey.

Williams

F1 entry:	**1978**
Races/Victories:	**379/104**
Drivers' Championships:	**7**
Constructors' Championships:	**9**
Pole positions:	**107**
Fastest laps:	**108**

The technology master of Grand Prix racing, Williams has enjoyed a consecutive seven-year run where its cars have generally been regarded as the fastest in the business. No-one has ever been the fastest for so long. That it has won 'only' four drivers titles during that time has been cited as evidence of a) not having the best drivers or b) its failings as a team. Frank Williams and partner Patrick Head have also been accused of being insensitive to the psychological needs of their drivers, causing them to under-perform. Whatever, it rather smacks of nitpicking with the team as current World Champions in both drivers' and constructors' contests.

Although Williams first entered F1 as a private entrant in 1969, it wasn't until 1977 that the current company began to take shape. That was when Frank was joined by designer Patrick Head and set up factory in Didcot, Oxfordshire. In Head's superb FW07 Clay Regazzoni took the team's first Grand Prix victory in 1979 and a year later Alan Jones took the World Championship with the car. Another title followed in 1982 with Keke Rosberg.

But these were the dying days of the 'kit car' where most of the teams simply plugged in a Cosworth DFV engine, designed a car around it and went racing. The turbo era changed all that and Williams made one of the best of all connections when it hooked up with Honda. It was during this time, in early 1986, that Frank Williams suffered a road accident which left him paralysed but which failed to dim his burning commitment to the team which carries his name. Head looked after shop during the convalescence and remarkably Williams was back in time to direct Nelson Piquet's 1987 World Championship.

Perhaps the title had taken longer coming than Honda expected but it was still a shock when the Japanese company announced that it would be transferring its allegiance to McLaren from 1988 onwards.

The short-term answer was a customer engine deal with Judd but 1989 saw the beginning of the longest and most successful partnership of the modern era - Williams-Renault. It was relatively successful straight off but took a couple of years to really hit form. From mid-'91 onwards though, the combination has been the one to beat, whether driven by Nigel Mansell (World Champion 1992), Alain Prost (ditto 1993), Damon Hill (1996) or Jacques Villeneuve (1997).

The 1997 FW19 was the last Williams design in which arodynamicist Adrian Newey had a hand before leaving for McLaren. The 1998 season will show whether Head and his design team have been able to bridge this gap seamlessly. The other cloud on the horizon is that Renault will no longer be involved on an official basis, though the same engines will be supplied by Mecachrome, the specialist company which has built the V10s for Renault all along. Longer term, the team has reached a partnership agreement with BMW for engine supply from 2000 onwards, but such natural structural changes often form the chink in the armour which sees a change in the order, a new era ushered in. Both McLaren and Ferrari are lined up waiting.

Benetton

F1 entry:	1986
Races/Victories:	251/27
Drivers' Championships:	2
Constructors' Championships:	1
Pole positions:	15
Fastest laps:	34

The team which took Michael Schumacher to consecutive world titles in '94 and '95, but which has had precious little success since the German ace departed to Ferrari. Owned by the Italian clothing company of the same name, the team has existed since 1986, its success before the Schumacher years being as sporadic as since. It has recently been through a fundamental personnel change and begins '98 with a clean sheet.

Benetton began with BMW engines in 1986, but switched to Ford for the next seven. Gerhard Berger had won its first triumph in Mexico that year, but over the ensuing years until 1994 it took only occasional Grand Prix wins and failed to launch a serious title bid. Some of this was down to Ford motors lacking sheer horsepower but there were fundamental organisational flaws in the team too.

Flavio Briatore came from elsewhere in the Benetton empire to run the show from 1989 but the solid foundations of the 1994/'95 championships really began to go down mid-way through 1991 when Ford approved of a deal for Tom Walkinshaw's TWR outfit to take a share in the team.

While Walkinshaw's structural changes were undoubtedly effective, he was helped in his cause by a couple of key personnel changes. Designer Rory Byrne had rejoined - he'd been working on the stillborn Reynard F1 project - at about the same time that John Barnard had left, unable to see eye-to-eye with the new regime. Concurrently, Walkinshaw brought with him TWR designer Ross Brawn. Brawn and Byrne formed a great working partnership but it was a late-season Walkinshaw swoop into the driver market that ultimately focused all this technical talent, and stands as Walkinshaw's greatest legacy to the team he left at the end of 1994. After making a sensational debut with Jordan at the 1991 Belgian Grand Prix, Michael Schumacher was snapped up and installed in a Benetton by the very next race. It caused an outcry at the time, but with hindsight it was the smartest single move in Benetton's history.

Schumacher went on to consecutive world titles with the team in 1994 and '95, with Ford and Renault power respectively. In an era of F1 where race strategy was becoming ever-more critical, the team earned an enviable reputation for invariably making the right calls. Partly this was down to Brawn getting the crew operating Saville Row slick, but much of it was simply a product of Schumacher's stunning speed giving the team a bigger envelope of possibilities in which to work.

Schumacher then left for the new challenge of Ferrari, ultimately taking both Brawn and Byrne with him. Benetton has won just one race since. There was to be one more departure: Briatore handed over the reigns late in 1997 to the Benetton family's appointee Dave Richards, the man whose Prodrive company had captured the World Rallying crown for Colin McRae and Subaru, but who is new to F1.

Pat Symonds and Nick Wirth are now the principal design brains and, after some highly promising stand-in performances for Berger in 1997, Alex Wurz has been recruited to partner comingman Giancarlo Fisichella in 1998. There's lot of potential there, but it's a very young team. Don't bet on any repeat of the Schumacher years for a while yet.

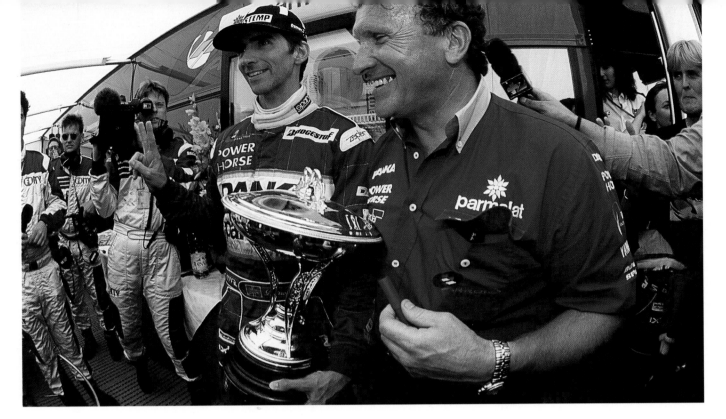

Arrows

F1 entry:	**1978**
Races/Victories:	**305/0**
Drivers' Championships:	**0**
Constructors' Championships:	**0**
Pole positions:	**1**
Fastest laps:	**0**

Formed in controversial circumstances 20 years ago, this team led its second Grand Prix yet has still to win one. It came awfully close in 1997 though, when Damon Hill lost the lead on the last lap of the Hungarian Grand Prix.

Founder member Jackie Oliver - former Lotus, McLaren and Shadow driver - is still a key figure in the team but since the start of 1996 the man in charge has been Tom Walkinshaw.

The brawny Scot, fresh from stints at Benetton and Ligier, represented the new era which would finally see Arrows come good after a lifetime of underachieving. He brought with him from Ligier designer Frank Dernie, moved the team to TWR's opulent Leafield base, took a Yamaha engine deal and Bridgestone tyres and for the 1997 season signed then-World Champion Damon Hill.

As yet the team's victory hopes remain just that and of those formative deals, only the re-siting of the factory and the Bridgestone tyres remain. Dernie left shortly after Walkinshaw hired John Barnard's services amid much disappointment over the performance of Dernie's A18 chassis. Hill has decided that another year in a still-developing team is not for him and the Yamaha's awful reliability and poor performance has led to its substitution by a Hart V10 with Yamaha badging.

On the plus side Barnard's changes to the car had a very positive effect, promising much for the future, and Hill's replacement is the excellent Mika Salo, keen to prove to the world what he already knows - that he's a potential Grand Prix winner. Backing him up will be Pedro Diniz, looking to build on a season in which he was expected to provide some money and nothing more but in which he impressed by occasionally outqualifying Hill.

There is almost certainly still some juggling and fixing of the basic elements for Walkinshaw to do - a proper factory engine deal is the obvious gap - but, given his past track record, it would be surprising if, long term, success is not on the way.

Jordan

F1 entry:	1991
Races/Victories:	114/0
Drivers' Championships:	0
Constructors' Championships:	0
Pole positions:	1
Fastest laps:	1

Wheeler-dealer, joker, loveable rogue are some of the terms habitually used to describe Irishman Eddie Jordan. But among such casual qualities there must be a core of steel, for the Jordan team has defeated all the odds by entering F1 in the 1990s without the support of a manufacturer, and remaining afloat, indeed prospering. It's now, together with Prost, knocking on the door of the 'big-four' teams.

Former racer Jordan - whose team won an F3 title with Johnny Herbert in 1987 and the F3000 crown with Jean Alesi in 1989 - made the graduation to the big time in 1991 with a tight little team, a customer engine and a neat chassis. That its performance was instantly credible was down to the talents of the team's technical director Gary Anderson, who has produced a series of good-handling Jordans ever since.

The progression from these promising beginnings to the team which in 1997 was in with a sniff of the odd race win on merit has not been a smooth one. The big breakthrough though, was the signing of a partnership deal with Peugeot in 1995, once the French manufacturer had been dumped unceremoniously by McLaren.

This not only gave Jordan some desperately needed financial stability, but an increasingly competitive engine. The 1995 motor was prodigiously fast though its power delivery was so sudden it tended to upset the balance of the car, while the 1996 chassis lacked downforce. With all this attended to in 1997 - and significant investment made in the technical facilities at the team's Silverstone base - Jordan was in its best-ever shape and came close to victory in both Argentina and Germany.

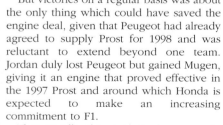

But victories on a regular basis was about the only thing which could have saved the engine deal, given that Peugeot had already agreed to supply Prost for 1998 and was reluctant to extend beyond one team. Jordan duly lost Peugeot but gained Mugen, giving it an engine that proved effective in the 1997 Prost and around which Honda is expected to make an increasing commitment to F1.

Theoretically this puts Jordan on pole position for an alliance with one of modern F1's super-powers. Which therefore makes its performances in 1998 critical to its long-term stature. In a bid to shore up a driving strength which last year had plenty of speed but little experience, Damon Hill joins Ralf Schumacher. Such winning experience could prove Jordan's final jigsaw piece.

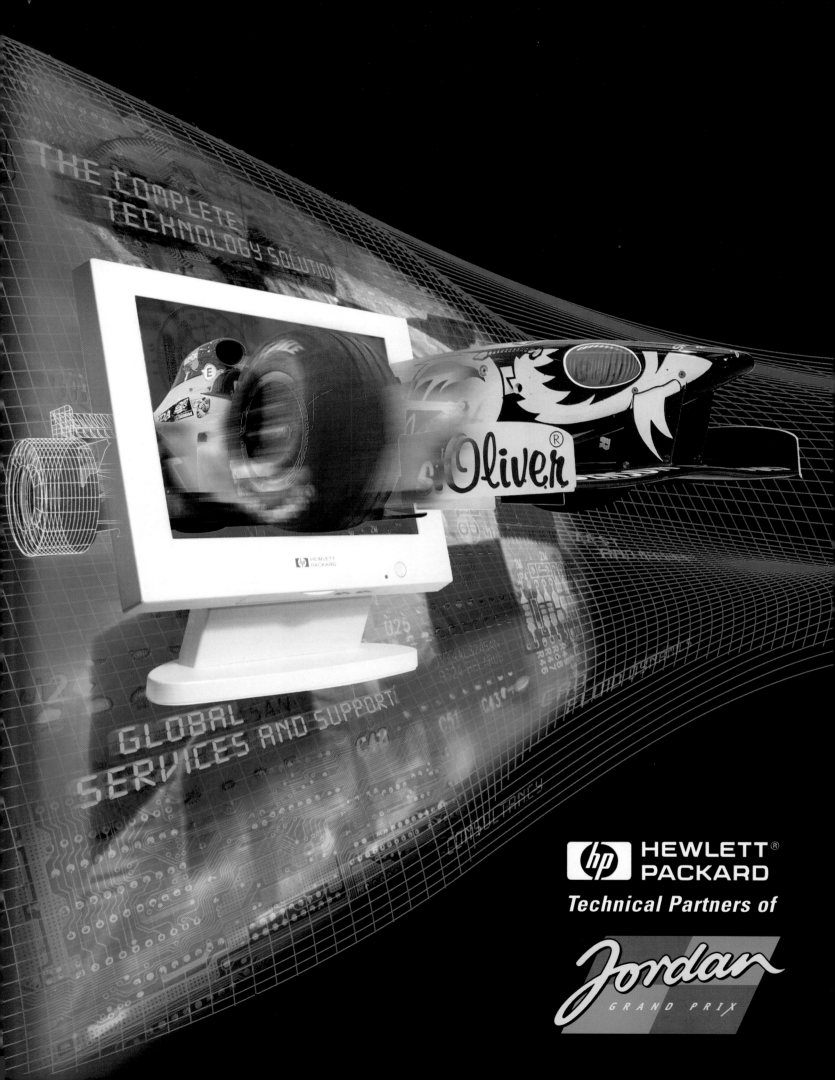

THE COMPLETE
TECHNOLOGY SOLUTION

s.Oliver®

HEWLETT®
PACKARD

GLOBAL SAN
SERVICES AND SUPPORT

Technical Partners of

Jordan
GRAND PRIX

Minardi

F1 entry:	**1985**
Races/Victories:	**205/0**
Drivers' Championships:	**0**
Constructors' Championships:	**0**
Pole positions:	**0**
Fastest laps:	**0**

Affectionately considered as F1's minnow team, Minardi keeps chugging along, just as it has since entering the game in 1985. It has in the last couple of seasons acted as a sort of holding team for young driving talent, both Giancarlo Fisichella and Jarno Trulli having served their time there until being called up by Flavio Briatore to graduate to the big league.

This has came about through then-Benetton boss Briatore taking a share in the team a couple of years ago, although the link has now been severed, with Briatore leaving F1 and selling his share in Minardi to Gabriele Rumi, who is now the main shareholder. Rumi first became involved as a partner with Minardi shortly after his own F1 team, Fondmetal, closed its doors in 1992.

Team founder Giancarlo Minardi remains on board, the man who took his little Faenza-based outfit into F1 after some F2 success in the late Seventies and early Eighties. Finances - usually sourced only in Italy - have never been comparable with the top teams and Minardi has always been obliged to cut his team's cloth accordingly. Nonetheless, there have been some moments of glory, notably with Pierluigi Martini -who sat on the front row of the grid at Phoenix in 1990, thanks largely to the effectiveness of his Pirelli qualifying tyres when the top teams were all on Goodyears.

This sort of form got the team an engine deal in 1991 - from Ferrari. Despite Martini chasing Alesi's Ferrari for third place at Estoril, however, the arrangement didn't last into a second year and thereafter it was back to an assortment of customer engines.

When an agreed Mugen deal for 1995 went instead to the Ligier team in which Briatore and Benetton had a stake, Giancarlo Minardi took legal action. The claims and counter-claims ended ultimately with Briatore making his investment in the team. His departure comes following stories of a rift after he failed to persuade Rumi and Minardi to sell out to the American BAT consortium, a deal that eventually went Tyrrell's way.

Without this link to a top team, and with only customer Ford engines to rely on, the way ahead for this small team is unclear. It continues into 1998 with Ford V10 engines, a further evolution of its Gabriele Tredozi chassis and its Bridgestone tyres.

F1 Racing SIMULATION

**OFFICIAL FIA WORLD CHAMPIONSHIP PRODUCT
DEVELOPED WITH RENAULT F1 ENGINEERS**

PC ZONE Classic

93% "Superb"

- 22 drivers, teams and cars from the '96 Championship
- Thrilling split screen multiplayer action
- Up to 8 players over a network
- Customiseable cars, pit stops and TV replays

FORMULA 1 RACING WHEEL

93% Ultimate PC

Get closer to the action!

Ubi Soft Entertainment Ltd., Vantage House, 1 Weir Road, Wimbledon, London SW19 8UX
Tel: 0181 944 9000 • Fax: 0181 944 9400 • e-mail: general@ubisoft.co.uk
http://www.ubisoft.co.uk

Copyright 1998 Ubi Soft Entertainment Ltd. All Rights Reserved. Licensed by Formula One Administration Limited. Windows '95 ® is a registered Trademark of Microsoft Corporation.

THRUSTMASTER®

Prost

F1 entry:	**1976**
	(as Ligier, 1997 as Prost)
Races/Victories:	**343/9**
Drivers' Championships:	**0**
Constructors' Championships:	**0**
Pole positions:	**9**
	(as Ligier)
Fastest laps:	**11**
	(as Ligier)

Quadruple World Champion Alain Prost finally became a team owner in 1997 after several years of trying. With backing from the French government he acquired the former Ligier team, complete with its deals for Mugen-Honda engines and Bridgestone tyres. He then sought and received permission to change its name, thus bringing to an end the marque which had graced the Grand Prix grids since 1976, often as France's only representative.

Though its history had been interspersed with moments of glory, there had never looked any real likelihood of sustaining success despite budgets that were often considerable. The siting of the team in France away from the mainstream of F1,

and the volcanic temperament of team founder Guy Ligier saw to that.

Prost, sacked from Ferrari and temporarily retired as a driver was, during the 1991-'92 off-season, interested in setting up a French 'superteam' and was steered in the direction of taking over Ligier. Unable to get the guarantees he sought, either from financial backers or the team itself, Prost turned his back on the deal and went on to his final World Championship in 1993 with Williams. But he would be back. On his own terms.

Ligier retired at the end of 1992 and after a transition period of ownership by Cyril de Rouvre (former owner of the small AGS team), a major stake was acquired in it by Benetton's man Flavio

Briatore, who remained until the Prost takeover.

The legacy of the Briatore era was the 1995 car, which was based very much on the World Championship-winning Benetton. This has remained the basis of the team's cars since, including the JS45 which wore the Prost badge in 1997 and showed so well in the hands of Olivier Panis and Jarno Trulli. Aided by a probable tyre advantage, the cars twice looked capable of winning on merit, a superb start for a new team owner.

Now the man who has steadily developed the car, Loic Bigois, is working on his first complete design, into which will be inserted the newly-acquired Peugeot engines. Much will rest on the effectiveness of that car.

Sauber

F1 entry:	1993
Races/Victories:	81/0
Drivers' Championships:	0
Constructors' Championships:	0
Pole positions:	0
Fastest laps:	0

This was the team which was earmarked for Mercedes' re-entry into Grand Prix racing, first appearing in 1993 with a Mercedes-badged Ilmor engine and a car bearing the legend 'concept by Mercedes-Benz'. However the German company then transferred its allegiance to McLaren, leaving its former partner to manage first with a Ford deal and, in 1997, a technical alliance with Ferrari which entailed the use of its engines badged in recognition of sponsor Petronas.

Prior to the Swiss team's F1 debut, team boss Peter Sauber had spent seven years building up his relationship with Mercedes in sportscar racing. Initially it built an engine for him then took a more active role in the development of the team, culminating in World Sports Car Championships for cars which by then wore the full Mercedes 'silver arrows' livery. It was the programme which ultimately awoke the sleeping giant to international motor racing after a very long absence.

If the graduation to F1 was natural, then so was the subsequent split after two seasons of only semi-competitiveness. Had there been prospects of imminent success, the partnership in all likelihood, would have continued. Instead, Mercedes naturally sought out a known quantity of a team, and none was better known than McLaren.

Although another engine partnership was quickly found in Ford - on the rebound from Benetton - its motors lacked ultimate horsepower. Furthermore, Ford informed the team that priority would be given in 1997 to the new Stewart project to which it was umbilically linked. It was time for a change, something merely confirmed when Heinz-Harald Frentzen - with Sauber, on and off, since the sportscar days - left the team headed for Williams.

Johnny Herbert was thus promoted to team leader and with Leo Ress' Ferrari-engined C16 enjoyed a moderately competitive year, though the car clearly disliked bumpy circuits. For the future, the team intends to use the Ferrari engine as a base for its own unit - an ambitious aim - and in the meantime has signed as Herbert's partner Jean Alesi, a man with more than a little experience of Ferrari motors. ●

Stewart

F1 entry:	**1997**
Races/Victories:	**17/0**
Drivers' Championships:	**0**
Constructors' Championships:	**0**
Pole positions:	**0**
Fastest laps:	**0**

Jackie Stewart, like Alain Prost, was a multiple World Champion driver who made the plunge into F1 team ownership in 1997. The similarity really ends there, for Stewart's was a from-scratch brand new team rather than the re-badging of an existing one. Given that is was a standing start rather than a rolling one, Stewart Grand Prix enjoyed an excellent debut season.

Stewart's avowed targets for 1997 were modest ones - a championship point - and they were well and truly exceeded in a season crowned by Rubens Barrichello's remarkable second place at Monaco.

Designed by former Arrows man Alan Jenkins, the Stewart SF1 was a neat but conventional chassis, powered by Ford's new Cosworth V10 and enjoying the benefits of Bridgestone tyres. These were widely believed to have a small but significant advantage in some circumstances over the Goodyears used by the top teams. The Ford was lacking pure top-end horsepower and in an effort to overcome this an exhaustive development programme meant that the testing was being done in public and there were lots of smoky blow-ups. Such is the price of progress.

Although Stewart maintains that he felt obliged to join in the chase to sign Damon Hill in the build-up to the season, he claims he was relieved it didn't happen as he wasn't sure the team would have been ready to handle the attendant pressure of expectation. Instead he settled on the pairing of Barrichello and Jan Magnussen, the first a former shooting star who had seemingly burned out prematurely, the other a novice touted by Stewart as having Senna-like potential.

With Stewart's empathy for the psychological needs of a driver, he immediately had Barrichello performing to his full potential, this the first time in a five-year F1 career that the Brazilian has looked to have the mental approach to match his speed. The problems with Magnussen took longer to sort - most of the season in fact. It took that long before the Dane looked a match for his team-mate, Stewart blaming bad habits picked up in Touring Cars.

In the calm, measured approach, in the full trust each partner seems to have in the other and in the safe hands at the tiller, it is difficult to imagine Stewart Grand Prix not eventually achieving its goals. It will probably be two or three years from now though.

Tyrrell

F1 entry:	**1968**
	(with Matra)
Races/Victories:	**402/23**
(435/33 including '68-'69 with Matra	
and '70 with March)	
Drivers' Championships:	**3**
(I running Matras; 2 as Tyrrell)	
Constructors' Championships:	**2**
(1 running Matra; 1 as Tyrrell)	
Pole positions:	**14**
(17 including Matra and March)	
Fastest laps:	**20**
(28 including Matra and March)	

its own car, the V12 engine for which was behind schedule. Tyrrell approached the company with the suggestion of him running a separate team for Stewart using the Ford Cosworth DFV which had made such an impact in its debut season of 1967. It was a blindingly obvious solution for Matra, but only Tyrrell had suggested it. Matra said yes, Stewart was immediately in contention for the world title and won it in '69.

It scored two points in 1997, courtesy of Mika Salo's 5th place at the drenched Monaco race. This involved a quick recognition that the race would conclude with a time limit rather than a distance one and so the planned fuel stop could be abandoned. It was the sort of on-the-feet thinking that Tyrrell has always specialised in. It's a pity Williams didn't employ him that day.

The team has now been bought out by

A team whose glory years - ironically with Jackie Stewart - are now a long-distant memory, Tyrrell saw out 1997 outgunned in the power stakes, with just a customer Ford motor. The slide began long ago and showed no sign of halting in the team's penultimate season - in 1999 it is to be absorbed by the new British American Tobacco superteam.

Most of Tyrrell's success was tied up with Stewart, the driver he first ran in F3 in the early 1960s. While Stewart had made the graduation to F1 as a driver by '65, Tyrrell continued to run him in F2 and saloon car events and they came together in F1 in '68.

French sports car manufacturer Matra was about to enter Grand Prix racing with

Quick-acting and well-organised, Tyrrell was a great team manager and just the sort of foil Stewart needed as a driver, someone he trusted implicitly to take care of all the small details which can lose a race. After the Matra years, and after a short period with customer March chassis, Tyrrell was established as a constructor in its own right. And Stewart continued to win in the rugged and effective cars with the simple, no-nonsense team patron.

Stewart won 25 Grands Prix for Tyrrell in six years. Since the Scot retired 24 years ago, Tyrrell has won eight times, and the last of these was in 1983. In an era of F1 that has increasingly required more than just common sense and hard work, Tyrrell has fallen behind.

the British American Tobacco conglomerate in a deal organised by Jacques Villenueve's manager, Craig Pollock and involving production race car constructor Reynard. This will take full effect from 1999, when the team will be re-sited to a new factory at Reynard's Bicester base and renamed British American Racing (BAR). With formidable financial backing, Reynard will pen the new car, with the stated ambition of winning the first Grand Prix of the 1999 season.

An era came to an end at the beginning of the '98 season when Ken Tyrrell resigned from the team following a disagreement over drivers. F1's most respected elder statesman was sorely missed.

Into The Future

In the uniquely competitive environment that is Formula 1, an essential component for any winning team is the ability to accelerate cycle times and be able to make decisions quickly.

CAD/CAM is the generic term for those computer systems which create and simulate products in three dimensions, cutting down drastically on development time and costs. A market leader in this field is the French company Dassault Systemes and its CATIA Solutions system.

It was in aeronautic design that Dassault Aviation, Dassault Systemes' parent company, first used CAD/CAM. To begin with, CATIA was exclusively an in-house resource of Dassault Aviation, but CATIA was put on a more serious footing when, in 1981, Dassault Systemes was created to develop the software.

Its use quickly spread from the aircraft industry and today CATIA plays a crucial

Photo courtesy of Peugeot

The Prost Peugeot AP 01

role in aerospace, consumer goods, shipbuilding, plant design, heavy machinery and the automotive industry and is widely used throughout the technological pinnacle of automotive design, Formula One. Computer giant IBM has a business partnership with Dassault Systmes for the CATIA system, and is licensed to sell it. Dassault Systemes now boasts 106,000 CATIA workstations and 10,000 customers.

The entire life-cycle of a part from concept to operation, including maintenance, can be simulated - all before making a single prototype. The design can thus be perfected before expensive and time-consuming manufacture begins. An entire product - even something as complex as an aircraft - can be designed and assembled in this virtual reality world. Boeing recently celebrated the completion of its first 100% digitally-designed aircraft, the 777, featuring three million CATIA-designed parts. Had the information generated by this project been stored on conventional 3.5-inch diskettes, 2.3 billion

of them would have been required !

In the automotive world, CATIA is used by Mercedes, BMW, Audi, Volkswagen, Chrysler, Honda, Fiat, Renault, Peugeot, Porsche, Mitsubishi, Volvo, Saab and Daewoo. With its Neon model, Chrysler set a record time of 31 months from initial concept to production, largely thanks to CATIA.

Apart from time and cost savings, there is also a great communication benefit. With the diversity of operations and skills in the design of a modern car, there is an inevitable tendency for the project to become somewhat abstract to those involved. Chrysler in particular has found that CATIA goes a long way to redressing this, allowing project members to more fully understand the processes and monitor progress by using the 'CATIA television'. Simultaneous development in different areas also becomes very much easier.

With the speed of technological change in Formula One racing, the benefits of such a system are obvious. Ferrari, Sauber, Cosworth, Honda, Renault Sport, Peugeot Sport, Bridgestone and Prost all utilise it, the last-named enjoying a full technical partnership with Dassault Systemes.

The Prost-Peugeot AP01 has been entirely digitally designed, with designer Loïc Bigois noting that the car's all-new gearbox, involving the design and manufacture of three separate casings took less than four months. "In the past this would have taken us eight months," he commented. The Peugeot V10 engine used by Prost for the first time in 1998 was itself digitally designed on CATIA - albeit separately from the car - and so the troublesome process for a designer of

Picture courtesy of Boeing

Design of the Boeing 777

adapting to a new engine has been eased considerably.

This, however, is just the beginning. With Prost, Dassault Systemes is looking to arrive at the point where not only will all the 3,000 parts making-up a F1 car be CATIA-designed but also those working on the design of even the smallest component will be able to access a digital mock-up of the entire car. Bills of material, pricing, fabrication plans, production planning needs and machining information with automatically proposed tolerances will all be incorporated into the system. CATIA will even design the machine tools required to make the components which it has simulated.

Bernard Dudot, Technical Director of Prost Grand Prix, comments: " It will allow us to optimise our processes and in the future we will be able to design our cars more quickly and earlier in the season."

In the spiralling intensity of F1 development, the system will be a major factor in Prost Grand Prix's achievement of its aim to become one of the sport's elite superteams.

DAIMLERBENZ
AKTIENGESELLSCHAFT

CATIA·CAD
SOLUTIONS

Photo courtesy of Daimler Benz